THE ART OF LEGAL PROBLEM SOLVING

A CRIMINAL LAW APPROACH

Legal reasoning is a critical aspect of the legal profession that is often overlooked or taught in overly simplistic ways. *The Art of Legal Problem Solving: A Criminal Law Approach* is a sophisticated skills book designed to help students develop the problem-solving techniques necessary for their legal careers.

This succinct yet comprehensive book provides the perfect mix of general instruction and specific examples to encourage students to think about problems both in depth and broadly. It follows a clear roadmap presented in a logical progression, beginning with the fundamentals, fact finding and statutory interpretation before turning to the advanced areas of analysing and writing answers to problem questions. While written primarily for criminal law students, the skills imparted are generic and can be applied equally in any area of the law and in any jurisdiction.

Incorporating over 15 years of teaching experience, *The Art of Legal Problem Solving* is an indispensable work for law students who want to not only improve their problem-solving skills but master them.

Brendon Murphy is Professor of Law at the School of Law, Southern Cross University.

Cambridge University Press acknowledges the Australian Aboriginal and Torres Strait Islander peoples of this nation. We acknowledge the traditional custodians of the lands on which our company is located and where we conduct our business. We pay our respects to ancestors and Elders, past and present. Cambridge University Press is committed to honouring Australian Aboriginal and Torres Strait Islander peoples' unique cultural and spiritual relationships to the land, waters and seas and their rich contribution to society.

THE ART OF LEGAL PROBLEM SOLVING

A CRIMINAL LAW APPROACH

Brendon Murphy

CAMBRIDGE
UNIVERSITY PRESS

CAMBRIDGE
UNIVERSITY PRESS

Shaftesbury Road, Cambridge CB2 8EA, United Kingdom

One Liberty Plaza, 20th Floor, New York, NY 10006, USA

477 Williamstown Road, Port Melbourne, VIC 3207, Australia

314–321, 3rd Floor, Plot 3, Splendor Forum, Jasola District Centre, New Delhi – 110025, India

103 Penang Road, #05–06/07, Visioncrest Commercial, Singapore 238467

Cambridge University Press is part of Cambridge University Press & Assessment, a department of the University of Cambridge.

We share the University's mission to contribute to society through the pursuit of education, learning and research at the highest international levels of excellence.

www.cambridge.org
Information on this title: www.cambridge.org/9781009778220

First published 2024
First paperback edition 2026

Cover designed by Simon Rattray, Squirt Creative

A catalogue record for this publication is available from the British Library

A catalogue record for this book is available from the National Library of Australia

ISBN 978-1-009-77822-0 Paperback
ISBN 978-1-009-45792-7 Epub

CONTENTS

About the author *page vii*
Acknowledgements *viii*

1 Introduction **1**
The art of problem solving 1
Beyond acronyms 2
Legal and ethical answers 3
The scope of this book 6

2 Fundamentals of problem solving **7**
Law as an applied predictive discipline 7
The relationship between law and evidence 8
How much law? 9
Choice of law determines the elements of proof 11
The iceberg principle 13
The role of evidence 15
Evidence is essential to the application of law 16
The elements of the offence 17
The hidden law in the elements 20
Key points 23

3 Fact finding **24**
Using evidence principles to think about facts 24
Sources of evidence 30
The burden of proof 35
The standard of proof 38

4 Statutory interpretation and the criminal law **42**
General principles 42
Interpretation Acts 44
Special rules and principles that apply to criminal statutes 45

5 Analysing a problem **55**
Basic problem analysis 55
Advanced problem analysis 58
Tentative conclusion 66

6 Putting it all together **68**
Apply law to facts, or facts to law? 68
Jurisdiction 68
Identify the harms and procedures 70
Scope the law 71

Identify the elements of the proposed offence 72
Preliminary interpretation 76
Identify the evidence 79
Associate and evaluate the elements and the evidence 82
Reject the weak, embrace the strong 86
Resolve factual uncertainties 86
Resolve legal uncertainties 89
Defence(s) 89
Alternatives 91
Procedural considerations 92
Sentencing 94
Tentative conclusion 95

7 Writing it up **97**
Purpose and audience 97
Format 98
Attend to the writing process 99
Engage with the law 100
Guiding principles 101

Appendix A: Hypothetical example problem 1 *103*
Appendix B: Hypothetical example problem 1 guided response *105*
Appendix C: Hypothetical example problem 2 and guided response *114*
Appendix D: Hypothetical example problem 2: Memorandum of advice in the matter of DPP v Ray Smith *118*
Index *123*

ABOUT THE AUTHOR

Dr Brendon Murphy is Professor of Law at the School of Law, Southern Cross University. He has served as Associate Professor at the Thomas More Law School, Australian Catholic University, and at Canberra Law School, Senior Lecturer at the University of Newcastle and Foundation Lecturer at the University of the Sunshine Coast. Prior to joining the academy in 2007, he worked as an in-house solicitor for the University of Newcastle, and in litigation in Newcastle after being admitted as a legal practitioner in the NSW Supreme Court.

Dr Murphy was awarded a Citation for Excellence in Teaching by the Australian Teaching and Learning Council and a Vice Chancellor's Award for Outstanding Contributions to Student Learning. He brings over 15 years' experience as an academic to his work. His research work straddles criminal law and procedure, investigations law and regulation, research methodology, policing and the intersection of law and social theory. He has published widely, including in the *Australian Criminal Law Journal*, *International Journal of Evidence and Proof*, *Griffith Law Review* and *Queens Law Journal*.

ACKNOWLEDGEMENTS

This book is dedicated first and foremost to my students, from whom I have learned a great deal over the years. They have obliged me to learn to laugh at myself and in doing so have kept me young at heart. I am constantly humbled by their courage. Most importantly, they have helped in crystallising the ideas behind this book.

My thanks extend to my professional colleagues with whom I have worked, both as teachers and friends. I particularly thank Associate Professor Kate Lindsay and Professor John Anderson, both of whom are model educators and outstanding teachers of the law. I am also indebted to Professor Simon Bronitt for early lessons in cultivating empathy, and Professor Patrick Keyzer, whose early work on problem solving started my own journey 23 years ago.

Sincere thanks to the production team at Cambridge for their hard work, especially Lucy Russell and Emily Baxter, and to the anonymous reviewers whose helpful suggestions shaped the book.

Finally, I am nothing without my family. I am grateful for my daughter, who thinks like me. For my son, who does not. And for my wife, who knows what windmills to charge at.

The author and Cambridge University Press would like to thank the following for permission to reproduce material in this book.

Figure 3.1: Simon Bronitt and Bernadette McSherry, *Principles of Criminal Law* (Thomson Reuters, 4th ed, 2017). Reproduced with permission of Thomson Reuters (Professional) Australia Limited, legal.thomsonreuters.com.au.

Extracts from *He Kaw Teh v The Queen* (1985) 157 CLR 523; *R v Youssef* (1990) 50 A Crim R 1: Reproduced with permission of Thomson Reuters (Professional) Australia Limited, legal.thomsonreuters.com.au.

Extracts from *Saad v R* (1987) 70 ALR 667: Originally published by LexisNexis.

Extracts from New South Wales legislation: Sourced from the New South Wales Legislation website at 10 August 2023. For the latest information on New South Wales Government legislation please go to https://www.legislation.nsw.gov.au. Reproduced under a CC BY 4.0 licence: https://creativecommons.org/licenses/by/4.0/.

INTRODUCTION

1

The art of problem solving

The discipline of law is unique as a body of knowledge. It is both theoretical and applied. Abstract and concrete. Moral and amoral. Just and cruel. And at its heart is a moment in which the abstract is translated into concrete action, a process that depends on theoretical application to the physical world. That application is linked to the art of problem solving.

Human beings are problem-solving animals. All of us possess skills and experiences that enable us to engage with obstacles and problems in life. A 'problem' is characterised by some event, experience or situation where our usual methods of operating and achieving desired ends are slowed down, prevented from operating, or simply no longer work in that environment. Failure to successfully navigate a problem creates a crisis, during which we engage in different forms of conduct and thinking to find a resolution. Crises operate on a spectrum. Some are life-threatening. Some are innocuous. But the underlying dynamic is much the same. Problem solving is an adaptive and evolved trait that humans share with other animals and that enables us to survive in changing environments.

In the context of education, learning how to apply knowledge presents a form of crisis. The initial reaction is stress, sourced from (1) knowing we must perform, (2) not knowing what we don't know without study and feedback and (3) being evaluated by those in authority. For law students this is all too familiar. Most people do not have any real experience with the law. But when they do, they are confronted by an environment that requires mobilisation of people, institutions and rule systems manifested in words and practices that stand outside ordinary experience. Working effectively in this environment requires years of training and education. It involves a form of reasoning in uncertainty.

Legal training is linked to the practitioner being able to mobilise the coercive power of the courts and associated processes in service of their client. Providing advice is fundamental to lawyering. In many cases that process is not an issue. There is a known set of facts, a clear and unambiguous body of law, and a predictable outcome. But in other cases the known elements are less clear, with an unpredictable outcome. In both cases the practitioner is making decisions and conclusions based on evaluation and application of law to known facts. This is one of the *essential* skills of the lawyer, and at its heart is a form of reasoning we call 'problem solving'.

Accordingly, one of the most important skills for a legal practitioner to learn is the ability to problem solve. By *problem solving,* I mean the ability to look at a body of information and law and make an evaluation about the likely legal issues arising from a given set of facts, as well as how the relevant law might apply in that situation in order to provide some certainty about the legal outcome. In other words, *it is the ability to analyse evidence and interpret law, and then apply the law to the available facts, and to do so in ways that accord with the nebulous idea of justice and provide an accurate prediction of likely outcome if considered by a court.*

Problem solving is an art form, as opposed to a mathematical exercise. It is true that there is a certain logical progression involved in problem solving in simple cases, but in complex cases legal reasoning is not a simple exercise in logic or algebra. Aspects of problem solving involve simple common sense and ordinary reasoning. However, because we are talking about *legal* problem solving, it is an exercise that can only be mastered through a broad and deep understanding of the relevant law, the availability of credible and admissible evidence, an understanding of the processes in which the law is being applied, and the ability to both interpret and apply the relevant legal principles in a specific context. Legal problem solving is a learned skill introduced to students earlier in their study of the law, and is practised regularly throughout one's career, to the point where it becomes a routine part of professional skill and knowledge. But it begins in law school.

Beyond acronyms

This book is written primarily for law students who are learning the art of legal problem solving. But it will also be of use in the analysis of hard cases by legal practitioners. The focus of this book is on the criminal law, particularly as it operates in New South Wales. However, the skills involved are generic and can be applied equally in any area of the law and in any jurisdiction. The principles are fundamentally applicable in all cases. And the reason for that is what we are concerned with is a form of *reasoning* as opposed to demonstrating expertise in one area of law or jurisdiction. It is a form of reasoning entrenched in the common law tradition.

A great deal has been written about problem solving and judicial reasoning, including books aimed at introductory and beginners' level of analysis,[1] through to more detailed works concerned with integrating legal problem solving with formal logic,[2] and treatises on judicial reasoning.[3] Despite the deep scholarship in the field, problem solving is routinely taught through acronyms of relatively basic principles. In law these include 'CLEO',[4] 'CRARC'[5] and, in the Australian context, 'MIRAT'[6] and 'IRAC'.[7]

1 Patrick Keyzer, *Legal Problem Solving: A Guide for Law Students* (LexisNexis Butterworths, 2nd ed, 2003).
2 Kenneth Yin and Anibeth Desierto, *Legal Problem Solving and Syllogistic Analysis: A Guide for Foundation Law Students* (LexisNexis Butterworths, 2016).
3 Herbert Hart, *Essays in Jurisprudence and Philosophy* (Clarendon, 1983); Benjamin Cardozo, *Nature of the Judicial Process* (Yale University Press, 1921); Frederick Schauer, *Thinking Like a Lawyer: A New Introduction to Legal Reasoning* (Harvard University Press, 2009); John Farrar, *Legal Reasoning* (Thomson Reuters, 2010).
4 SI Strong, *How to Write Law Essays and Exams* (Oxford University Press, 5th ed, 2018).
5 Gerald Lebovits, 'Cracking the Code to Writing Legal Arguments: From IRAC to CRARC to Combinations in Between' (2010) 82(6) *New York State Bar Association Journal* 64.
6 John Wade, 'Meet MIRAT: Legal Reasoning Fragmented into Learnable Chunks' (1991) 2(1) *Legal Education Review* 283; Keyzer (n 1).
7 Robin Creyke et al, *Laying Down the Law* (LexisNexis, 11th ed, 2021).

The acronyms refer to basic steps in reasoning that aim to replicate broad steps in judicial reasoning. IRAC, for example, stands for 'Issue', 'Rule', 'Application' and 'Conclusion'. While the reasoning process involved in adjudication and analysis broadly covers those concepts, the model is problematic for several reasons. First, it implies a sequential logic from 'Issue' to 'Conclusion' and tends to result in novices fragmenting their analysis into distinct phases at the expense of the required level of reasoning, which is more of a synthesis than a structured sequence. Legal reasoning is not 'linear' – it requires the ability to move backwards and forward, spot intersections, determine uncertainties, resolve gaps, anticipate outcomes, evaluate concurrence, and so on. IRAC is problematic because it also suggests that that 'issues' will be immediately apparent – which they are not. Often it is only when the rule is being characterised and applied that the issue becomes clear. But the central problem with 'IRAC' and models like it is the simplistic nature of the concept, and its inability to integrate intersecting areas of law (such as evidence and procedure) and anticipate what to do next. While it is a basic, and useful, introductory framework for thinking about legal problem solving, it's problematic in terms of developing skill and knowledge about what to advise and how to act.[8]

Legal and ethical answers

This book offers an alternative approach, one that has emerged out of my own experiences in teaching the criminal law, and the application of it, over the last 15 years in various Australian universities. This methodology tries to make the process both comprehensive and nuanced, without the unnecessary trappings of formal logic, and resisting the temptation to oversimplify what is actually a very complicated process. In presenting this methodology in this book, I aim to articulate some of the nuances of legal reasoning in a way that captures the relevant complexities but does not get bogged down in formal syllogisms.

Most students who pick up a book on legal problem solving like this share something in common. They would like to learn the art of problem solving; and they are motivated by grades. *My first piece of advice is to forget the mark and focus on the process.* Marks follow the process. Attention to detail and pride in the work are the keys. Stressing about the product is a distraction. The second piece of advice is to remember that *you don't know what you don't know.* And the reason that is important is that you cannot properly engage with the task unless you know enough about it to be able to spot the relevant issues, deploy the relevant law and write it up in a manner that is purposeful and at a tertiary standard. Successful problem solving demands time devoted to knowing the law, and systematically working with it.

A further hurdle for students is the assumption there is a 'right answer'. The answer is 'it depends'. Unlike the sciences, law is characterised as a discipline that can, in some circumstances, have a definitive answer. It is also a discipline where there may *not* be a single 'correct' answer. It is a discipline of 'potentialities'. Legal reasoning has different forms, depending on the presence of certainty in fact and law. The combination of these

8 Jessica Slavin, 'Did You Learn About IRAC in Law School? How Did IRAC Become Such an Important Part of Legal Writing Teaching? And Should It Be?', *Marquette University Law School Faculty Blog* (online, 11 September 2008).

two aspects determines the kind of reasoning used. Broadly, when the facts and law are clear and certain, then legal reasoning is 'linear' – an almost mathematical answer. In these cases, there is no need for judicial determination because the outcomes are clear. But when fact and law are unclear, then legal reasoning changes complexion and becomes 'dextrous', moving across and within different categories to locate the point of uncertainty with an eye to predictive and settled application.[9] This will be discussed in more detail later on.

An answer may be considered 'wrong' when it is legally flawed. The reason I suggest that is that a legally flawed outcome presents significant issues for the client. They are unable to rely on the outcome, and there are attendant consequences. In a civil context, for example, there are cost implications in addition to the orders made in resolution of the dispute. In the criminal context, a person may be wrongly convicted, or not convicted of something they should be. Lawyers have a duty to the court, and that includes not allowing the judge to fall into appealable error. This is to be contrasted with an answer the client *does not like*. Indeed, it is an important part of lawyering to be able to both give news the person does not want to hear, and to advise on ways to mitigate or respond to adverse outcomes. In that context *bad advice* is to leave the person without options at all, or to provide options that, again, are legally flawed. These real-world outcomes are normally reflected in the grading of assessment tasks while at law school.

Let's consider a criminal law example. Let's assume that our client is factually guilty of a crime. Clearly the person's real interest lies in avoiding going to prison. After reviewing the brief, your advice is that the prospect of them being convicted is high. Not only that, but it is also likely that a prison term will be ordered. Your advice might be for your client to plead guilty and focus on ensuring due process and submitting a strong plea in mitigation. The aim is not to avoid a conviction, but to minimise the penalty. Here the answer is legally sound, but not in your client's personal interests if their ultimate goal was staying out of prison. They *do*, however, benefit from your advice because it has reduced their exposure to a greater penalty than might otherwise be the case. So, in this case the idea of competence is linked to sound legal outcomes, which may conflict with personal hopes.

Similarly, a prosecutor who fails in convicting an accused is not incompetent simply because the court decides the evidence does not reach the required standard of proof. An accused person is entitled to test the evidence against them in open court. Similarly, a defence lawyer is not incompetent simply because the accused gets convicted. Competent practice is linked to the legality of the proceedings and the extent to which the practitioner enables that process. Of course, professional practice *may* be incompetent and the primary cause of the result, but in such cases that outcome is routinely corrected by the appellate courts, and often with related sanction against the practitioner. Examiners will often note the answer is 'wrong' when it is not available in the law and fact matrix. Examples of incompetent process and outcomes include:

- mobilising the wrong law
- misinterpreting the law

9 For an excellent examination of this see Richard Fischl and Jeremy Paul, *Getting to Maybe: How to Excel in Law School Exams* (Carolina Academic Press, 1999).

- misreading the facts
- making assumptions not supported by the facts
- making conclusions unsupported by the facts
- telling clients what they want to hear rather than the truth.

Incompetent answers will also be *wrong* when the legal adviser has engaged in *unethical practice*. For example, it is perfectly legitimate to represent and advise a client in a situation where they are factually guilty but the testing of the evidence cannot establish the burden of proof. That is very different to advising a client to arrange a false alibi, for example. These instances may not only result in adverse results for the client, but *also* adverse outcomes for the practitioner, such as a professional sanction. Students may be tempted to engage in unethical practice and are firmly advised not to do so. Students engaging in unethical practice will normally face an administrative sanction that may result in exclusion from practice. Not only do they risk losing marks, failing courses and sometimes being expelled, but their conduct will also be a matter that must be disclosed to admitting authorities and may result in the student being refused admission to the profession. Examples of unethical practice potentially engaged in by lawyers and students include:

- plagiarism
- ghost writing
- misrepresenting the law
- making decisions to achieve personal goals
- using artificial intelligence (AI) software to generate answers (where that has been prohibited by the examiner).

As an example, consider the following practice scenario. A lawyer is prosecuting a matter in a Local Court[10] on a minor criminal offence. The opposing party has signalled instructions to plead guilty to the charge. The day before the matter is listed, the prosecutor discovers that the charge is subject to a limitation period that has expired. As a matter of law, liability for the offence has expired. How might we proceed? One option is to say nothing and proceed with the prosecution. The desire here is to secure a conviction, and to avoid the inevitable question as to why the prosecutor did not pick this up. What are the likely outcomes? First, the accused is pleading guilty to an offence that has expired. The conviction is unlawful. A few weeks later the accused appeals against conviction. The conviction is extinguished. The prosecutor is now exposed as having knowingly prosecuted a matter in breach of the law. There are adverse consequences for the client and the lawyer for unethical practice. Neither outcome is acceptable, so clearly the correct course of action would have been to alert the defendant, have the matter withdrawn, and learn from the experience to check the limitation dates well before the matter is before a court. The message for students is to always be mindful that *ethical practice* is a professional expectation of practitioners and students of the law. You will not learn the

10 This term is not in uniform use around the common law world. Some jurisdictions have Magistrates' Courts. This is a reference to courts of 'Petty Sessions', where matters are heard summarily and at first instance.

skill if you don't engage with it personally, ethically, and competently. And remember, your reputation in a profession is everything.

The scope of this book

This book provides guidance on learning to think about applied law in a sophisticated and nuanced way. Legal reasoning is a critical aspect of legal practice but tends to be taught in rather simplistic ways. This book presents a range of observations and practices that assist in developing problem-solving and legal reasoning skills by encouraging analysts to think about problems in depth and broadly. There is a degree of repetition throughout, partly because the origins of this book are in notes, but also because repetition is a useful learning tool. Chapter 2 introduces some of the fundamentals of problem solving as a key aspect of applied law. It is concerned with developing ideas around the relationship between law and evidence, and thinking about the network of concepts on the surface and hidden in the network of laws that apply to a given fact matrix. In Chapter 3 we turn to thinking about evidence, or fact finding, as a key aspect of legal reasoning, since in all cases the deployment of the law depends on the existence or non-existence of certain fact combinations. Because the establishment of 'fact' in law depends on the application of the rules of evidence, we use principles from the law of evidence to assist in thinking about facts. Chapter 4 extends our understanding of the elements of law through a consideration of the rules of statutory interpretation. In Chapter 5 we move to a more detailed review of analytical principles, before turning to the application of those principles in Chapter 6. Finally, the book concludes with a discussion on how to go about writing up your findings.

Readers will also find examples of the writing-up task in the appendices. Appendix A contains a hypothetical problem, while Appendix B provides an example discussion of the problem in Appendix A. The Appendix A scenario is the subject of discussion throughout the book. In addition, there is a second example problem that is responded to in both Appendices C and D. Each of these provides an example of different forms of presentation of a problem. Appendix C presents an example of how you might go about writing up a problem question/analysis, while Appendix D provides an example of a letter of advice on the same question.

FUNDAMENTALS OF PROBLEM SOLVING

2

Law as an applied predictive discipline

Law is an applied and theoretical discipline. To that end, the law must be applied to the facts available when assessing the alignment of the facts with the law. In this respect law is an *empirical* discipline, requiring objective fact and law in association with one another in its application. Evidence must exist to establish fact, while law must exist to establish the rule structure. The relationship between law and evidence is unique, for it is not simply the existence of objectively present objects that will establish the 'fact' – the 'fact' in law is subject to further legal construction through the laws of evidence. The parties can agree on the facts, which a court is likely to accept. But when the facts are in dispute, the 'facts' must be established by adducing evidence. One aspect of that process is that an object or event that has actual existence may not, as a matter of law, be available to the decision maker because of legal invalidity. Hence the empirical foundations of fact are based on *admissible* evidence, rather than mere evidence. This will be considered in more detail in Chapter 3.

At its simplest, there are three possibilities in any combination of law and fact: (1) the facts and law are aligned, meaning that the law clearly applies; (2) the facts and law are not aligned, meaning the law does not apply; and (3) overlapping with (2), the facts and/or law *may* apply, subject to further evidence or clarification on interpretation. This is discussed in more detail in Chapter 5.

Application, of course, requires isolation of operative terms and concepts in the language of the law expressed in legislation and case authorities. That process involves interpretation of those terms, which may be applied to or qualified by the facts of the case and the rules of interpretation.

In the context of the criminal law, the key issue normally relates to whether an accused person is guilty of an offence but may also involve questions about the legality of procedures. In more advanced analysis, it routinely involves questions linked to the admissibility and existence of evidence, coupled with the existence or non-existence of a defence. In other areas of law, the issues will be linked to elements of a cause of action, or the operative parts of legislation or case principles that also need to be considered in the interplay of law and fact.

The process of resolving these questions involves a complex process of identification of relevant law, the interpretation of it, and its application to the relevant, admissible evidence. This is done for a purpose, and that purpose is concerned with accurately anticipating the outcome of decisions in court. Here there are two kinds of decisions: (1) process decisions and (2) outcome decisions.

A process decision is made *during* the proceedings. An example might be a decision a judge makes relating to the admission of evidence. An outcome decision is made at the *conclusion* of proceedings. The decision maker may vary. Guilt or innocence is a question of fact determined by the tribunal of fact (which may be a judge or jury). Culpability and sentence are a mixed question of fact and law – this rests with the judicial officer. In that determination, the judicial officer relies heavily on the submissions and evidence adduced by legal practitioners during the trial. But what is often overlooked is the central role that legal practitioners play before the matter even gets to court.

Legal practitioners play a key role in the early phases of legal disputes and engage in what we might call 'non-judicial legal reasoning'. This form of reasoning is essentially predictive. The process involves a consideration of the available evidence, applied to the relevant law, that is directed towards predicting the most likely outcome if the matter were to proceed to judicial determination in a court. This activity is of significant value to clients because it enables decision making early in the process. In civil disputes it will enable decisions about whether to proceed with a case at all, the scope of potential settlement, and an appraisal of the significance of evidence. In criminal cases, it facilitates decisions on the appropriate charge, the merits of a guilty plea, elections on indictment, and an evaluation of evidence. *The central purpose of problem solving is to predict as accurately as possible the outcome of a scenario should the matter proceed to court.*

The problem-solving tasks involved vary, depending on the orientation of the assessor to the case. Where the charge is *known* (eg a specific charge is alleged in a *court attendance notice* or *indictment*), the analysis proceeds from that charge, but must also be alert to viable alternatives. Here the analysis proceeds from the law to the facts and back again. Where the charge is *unknown* (eg evidence of potential crime presents itself, but no charge has yet been identified), the analysis proceeds from the evidence towards the law and back again. These two positions are broadly reflective of the tasks engaged in by the defence and the prosecution respectively. As we will see, a skilled analyst will know how to approach a problem from both perspectives.

The relationship between law and evidence

Legal analysis is guided by two principles: (1) the *law* and (2) the *evidence*. The two are intimately connected. The evidence determines what law is engaged, and the extent to which it is engaged. However, the law will also give emphasis to different aspects of the evidence as being of greater or lesser importance. Within the architecture of law will be *operative terms* that must be identified and interpreted and, in some cases, characterised to determine the nature and scope of the governing norm (as in constitutional law). For example, s 51(xxxi) of the *Australian Constitution* enables the Commonwealth Parliament to acquire property on 'just terms'. The meaning of 'just terms' must be determined with reference to the existing jurisprudence (decided cases and ethical philosophy) as applied to the facts of the case. The concept of 'just terms' is one of the central components in reasoning, and hence an 'operative term'.

These operative terms are usually referred to as 'elements'. Whether the law being considered is criminal, civil or procedural, the governing principle is to begin by identifying the existence of operative terms within each statement of law. This is not necessarily easy, because (as mentioned above) it depends on having a sense of what the relevant law is at the outset, which may be known, or unknown, depending on the case. In many cases this is not controversial. The correct law is known or easily identified. In other cases, there may be a process of 'testing' the facts and law in order to identify what category of law applies in the context.

In the context of substantive criminal law, the elements of the offence/defence must be identified and interpreted to the extent necessary to evaluate whether or not the category applies in the case. The *extent necessary* really depends on whether there is something controversial about the law or the facts. Where the law and facts are clear and unambiguous, detailed elaboration is unnecessary.

For example, let's assume the accused has been charged with dangerous driving causing death. (In New South Wales this is an offence under s 52A(1) of the *Crimes Act 1900* (NSW).) The passenger of the vehicle was killed in a collision between two cars. In a simple case, the fact of *death*, and the fact the car is a *vehicle* within the meaning of s 52A(9) of the *Crimes Act*, do not need an essay. Someone is dead. They were in a car. These are elements of the offence. There is no issue in either law or fact in this case. That is something that can be clearly stated in a single sentence referring to the relevant law in a footnote.

But what happens when one variable is not so clear? Let's now assume that the passenger was riding on an e-scooter at the time of the accident. Now there is a live issue, because there is a new category that may or may not fall within the statutory definition of 'vehicle'. That would require discussion about whether the e-scooter falls within the meaning of 'vehicle'. Let's now consider a situation where the medical evidence is not clear about whether the person was already dead when the accident took place. Maybe the accident happened because the driver was racing the person to hospital? Now there is a *causation* question to consider. That requires analysis and discussion because there must be a causal link between the driving of the offender and the death. The point here is to adopt a flexible position if the categories being considered are novel or the facts trigger different analytical rules.

How much law?

Novices routinely ask 'How much law do I use?' or 'How many cases should I cite?'. The answer depends on the complexity of the problem, and the extent to which the authorities relied on provide a definite answer to the question. When considering the depth of law required, be guided by these rules:

- The law must be *accurate.*
- The law must be *relevant.*
- The law deployed must be appropriately *detailed.*

The first thing that always needs to be considered when deploying the law is its accuracy. You need to ensure that the source of law you are using is correct and up to date for the jurisdiction you are in. Accuracy is sometimes a problem for law students because they often refer to textbooks, or to simple electronic searching on the internet. They often rely on secondary sources. The difficulty is that law is dynamic, and even well-recognised and authoritative textbooks go out of date – sometimes rapidly. It is therefore important to ensure that even though you might have identified what you think is the right law in a text, you cross-check it. For example, refer to a current database containing the relevant legislation and cases to make sure that the legislation has not changed, and that you know of recent case developments. Doing so not only ensures accuracy, but it also demonstrates to the examiner that you care about accuracy and are aware of developments. These steps are not only important for learning as a student of law – they are critical in practice, for your submissions must be solid if they are to be accepted in court.

It sounds trite, but the law you deploy needs to be *relevant* to the task at hand. Even when you have identified the correct law, and the elements, as mentioned, it is simply unnecessary to discuss the intricacies of a legal term where there is no issue. For example, there is no need for a lengthy discussion on the definition of death in a hypothetical where a person is dead. The fact that a person is dead is rarely a fact in issue. However, if you had a hypothetical in which a person disappeared, then the question of death is relevant to discuss, and accordingly you would then engage in an appropriate level of discussion. So here remember that *relevance* is linked not only to what law applies in the case, but also the extent to which it needs to be discussed and considered. Where the evidence sits clearly within the conceptual category established by the law, a lengthy treatise is unnecessary.

This leads to the third point, which is about the incorporation of *appropriate detail.* What is appropriate? The appropriate amount of detail is a discussion about the law in sufficient breadth and depth to demonstrate command of the relevant concept and to convince the reader that your assessment is legally correct and can easily be checked through the accurate citation of credible sources. In other words, the amount of discussion is a matter of judgement based on the complexity of the problem and the extent to which you need to engage in persuasive argument. In the example above, the scenario was that a person's body was missing. If your factual matrix indicates that a person is dead, and there is a coroner's report and death certificate, then there is no need to engage in a lengthy discussion about death. However, repeating the point above, if the person had simply disappeared and there was no evidence of death, then it would be appropriate to engage in discussion on the relevant law that has considered cases where the body is missing and there is no clear evidence of death.

Depending on the facts, it may be that most of your discussion will revolve around this point as it will necessarily depend upon the presentation of a circumstantial case, which often requires an extensive consideration of case authorities. The point here is to decide about the amount of detail that is necessary in order to persuade the reader. Sometimes this will be brief, sometimes lengthy. This can be challenging in assignment work, as students are routinely presented with word limits to contain the extent of analysis to make examination easier for a marker who may be marking dozens, if not hundreds, of papers. In a discipline like law, word count is an important training mechanism, because you are not at liberty to engage in an endless discussion when doing advice work. Your client will not appreciate an unnecessarily verbose and hefty document when the answer to the question asked may simply be 'Yes', especially when they are being charged money for it. So, if your facts clearly state the victim is dead, there is no need to spend 500 words discussing the law and fact of death, because it is not a live issue. Save the word count for what matters.

Choice of law determines the elements of proof

The law you deploy is selected based on a set of variables. In some cases, the law you use is based on a decision to mobilise it. For example, in civil law or equity, this might be via an injunction. In the criminal law it might be via a charge or a defence. In other cases, the law is contextual, which means it will only apply in whatever context you are considering. For example, the rules of court and governing legislation will apply because you are operating in that context. Linked to the context are the rules linked to process, such as the laws of evidence. The laws that you will need to consider are therefore determined by the *source* of law relevant to the context and the extent to which that source provides clarity and authority on the issue. In most cases this source will be legislation, but as law is an interpretive discipline it may also involve references to cases, especially where the law is unclear and there are divergent authorities. Cases will have the effect of affirming the way legislation is interpreted, but may also qualify that interpretation (sometimes narrowly, sometimes broadly). Cases that are concerned with common law will often engage in a process of synthesising and explaining the *principle(s)* of law drawn from decided cases. Broadly, there will be choices you make on the law to consider, and other instances where that law will be imposed on the process and reasoning.

Example: Some basic statutory interpretation

Let's say your client, Eric, has been charged in relation to a fight outside a bar. The victim in this case suffered head injuries after being hit in the head during the fight and falling to the ground. The basic case is that Eric willingly participated in the fight but did not intend to cause the injury ultimately suffered by the victim.

Let's assume Eric is charged with 'reckless infliction of grievous bodily harm' pursuant to s 35(2) of the *Crimes Act 1900* (NSW). The decision to charge is at the discretion of the prosecutor, informed by prosecutions policy. The section provides:

> **(2) Reckless grievous bodily harm** A person who—
> **(a)** causes grievous bodily harm to any person, and
> **(b)** is reckless as to causing actual bodily harm to that or any other person,
> is guilty of an offence.
> Maximum penalty—Imprisonment for 10 years.

The starting point is to identify key parts of the section. The operative elements of the offence are what the prosecution must prove to convict Eric. These are sourced in the language of the section.

(2) **Reckless grievous bodily harm** A person who—

(a) causes grievous bodily harm to any person, and

(b) is reckless as to causing actual bodily harm to that or any other person,

is guilty of an offence.

Maximum penalty—Imprisonment for 10 years.

Here the operative elements of the offence are outlined: (1) a person; (2) causes; (3) grievous bodily harm; (4) recklessness; and (5) actual bodily harm. As we will learn, (1) and (2) are contextual, whereas (3), (4) and (5) are essential.

Essential elements

The essential elements are those that must be considered in every case and must be proven beyond reasonable doubt in criminal cases, or on the balance of probabilities in civil cases. We will discuss the elements of offences in more detail shortly. For present purposes, it is enough to note that, in the present example, the essential elements are that Eric must have caused grievous bodily harm and must have (at a minimum) been reckless as to causing actual bodily harm. In order to establish Eric's liability, we would need to interpret the meaning of the essential elements and consider the evidence in support of each. Establishing the meaning of those elements requires a consideration of defined terms, where they exist in legislation, the ordinary meaning of words in some instances, and the reasoning of judges in various cases. This process will be discussed in more detail later on.

Contextual elements

A 'contextual' element is one that may or may not be in issue. An 'essential' element is one that must apply in each case. Together with a penalty provision, these components form the essential structure of legislation. In the deep structure of legislation in the criminal law, these elements have common characteristics. In the common law, the essential elements were known as 'actus reus' and 'mens rea', the prohibited act and the culpable state of mind. In the various Codes, these are often referred to as *physical* and *fault* elements. These elements must be proven on the admissible evidence beyond reasonable doubt. Consequently, you will always be looking for evidence that satisfies the essential elements of the offence, including evidence that may trigger a contextual element.

Personality

Here we will start by thinking about contextual elements. The requirement that Eric is a 'person' is deceptively simple. As a matter of law, a 'person' includes both an ordinary human being, and a body corporate.[1] At its simplest, this is rarely an issue on its own. It merely means that it is technically possible to prosecute a body corporate for the offence under consideration (although that rarely happens outside of the workplace health and

1 See, eg, *Interpretation Act 1987* (NSW) s 21.

safety cases). However, this is a reminder to think about related and overlapping questions linked to *legal personality*. From a practical perspective, this is normally only ever an issue where the accused is a juvenile, especially if under 14 years of age. This will be flagged as a potential issue going forward. Personality is also based on the assumption that the person charged is the person who actually committed the offence. That is not always the case. Sometimes the identity of the person is a fact in issue, and in the context of offences involving multiple parties, the role of the accused in the event may also be a fact in issue.

Penalty

An important component here is the statutory maximum penalty. This tells us several things, which may not be apparent to the untrained eye. First, the statutory maximum is the *maximum* penalty for an offence of that kind. It is not a declaration of a penalty that applies to every case.[2] Second, the general common law principle is that maximum penalties are reserved for instances of the *worst kind* of offences of that category (providing a guide as to the penalty that might be imposed).[3] Third, the penalty that can be imposed points to questions concerned with jurisdiction. Students must always be thinking about which court has authority to impose penalties of the kind set in legislation, and whether there are hidden restrictions if the case is being dealt with in a lower court that has additional statutory limits on penalty. We will return to questions of jurisdiction later.

Causation

In addition to penalty and personality, there is an ancillary element linked to 'causation'. This requires that Eric is properly identified and has legal capacity to commit the offence, and that there is *some causal link* between the actions of Eric and the injury to the victim. That may or may not be an issue, depending on the facts of the case. In most cases causation is not an issue; there is usually obvious evidence that some action, omission or event caused the relevant harm. But where causation is an issue, there is a good deal of complexity in the law that must be considered.[4]

The iceberg principle

By now, you should be starting to get a sense that legal reasoning involves what might be described as the 'iceberg larceny principle'. That is, what you see is part of a much larger whole, much of which is below the surface – and often what floats beneath the sea is more important than what is above it. The same is true in legal reasoning. With that in mind, it is a fundamental principle of statutory interpretation that sections of legislation must be read as part of a whole. Consequently, our evaluation of s 35(2) in Eric's scenario must consider the whole section. In this case s 35 contains four *different* offence provisions *and* a statutory *alternative verdict*.

2 See, eg, *Crimes (Sentencing Procedure) Act 1999* (NSW) s 49.
3 See *Ibbs v The Queen* (1987) 163 CLR 447 and *Veen v The Queen (No 2)* (1988) 164 CLR 465.
4 See, eg, *Royall v The Queen* (1991) 172 CLR 378; *Leyland Shipping v Norwich Union Fire Insurance* [1918] AC 350; *Krakouer v Western Australia* (2006) 161 A Crim R 347; *Arulithakan v The Queen* (2003) 78 ALJR 257; *R v Pagett* (1983) 76 A Cr App R 279.

35 Reckless grievous bodily harm or wounding

(1) **Reckless grievous bodily harm—in company** A person who, in the company of another person or persons—

(a) causes grievous bodily harm to any person, and

(b) is reckless as to causing actual bodily harm to that or any other person,

is guilty of an offence.

Maximum penalty—Imprisonment for 14 years.

(2) **Reckless grievous bodily harm** A person who—

(a) causes grievous bodily harm to any person, and

(b) is reckless as to causing actual bodily harm to that or any other person,

is guilty of an offence.

Maximum penalty—Imprisonment for 10 years.

(3) **Reckless wounding—in company** A person who, in the company of another person or persons—

(a) wounds any person, and

(b) is reckless as to causing actual bodily harm to that or any other person,

is guilty of an offence.

Maximum penalty—Imprisonment for 10 years.

(4) **Reckless wounding** A person who—

(a) wounds any person, and

(b) is reckless as to causing actual bodily harm to that or any other person,

is guilty of an offence.

Maximum penalty—Imprisonment for 7 years.

(5) **Alternative verdict** If on the trial of a person charged with an offence against any subsection of this section the jury is not satisfied that the offence is proven but is satisfied that the person has committed an offence against any other subsection of this section (that carries a lesser maximum penalty), the jury may acquit the person of the offence charged and find the person guilty of an offence against that other subsection. The person is liable to punishment accordingly.

In some cases, it is necessary to consider the alternatives. For present purposes only s 35(2) is engaged, although there may be instances where other provisions are engaged, depending on the facts.

At this point we have identified the elements to be considered in respect of the section, but there are also hidden elements in *surrounding legalities*. The fact the stated penalty is imprisonment for 10 years suggests this is a *serious indictable offence*. Accordingly, we must also consider the procedural dimension of this charge to understand where the matter will be determined. Above we observed the question of jurisdiction. Jurisdiction is a common problem overlooked by many novices in criminal law assessment, as many offences are dealt with by Local/Magistrates' Courts although they are technically indictable and could be presented to a jury trial in the District/County Court. These matters invite consideration of the underlying (and hidden) procedural rules.

Then there is the question of *limitation periods,* where they exist. In civil law it is common for limitation periods to restrict taking action without leave of the court. In the criminal law, there are generally no limitation periods unless the category is a summary offence. But thinking about limitation periods is useful not only for whether there are legal impediments to bringing the action at all, but also for the law that may apply to a criminal charge. The general rule is that a person is liable for a criminal charge based on the law that applied to the conduct on the day in which the event took place. Further, thinking about limitation periods is applicable to important procedures that may be in play. For example, there are often important deadlines that need to be complied with in relation to the service of notices.

And finally, of no less importance, is the existence (or not) of a valid *defence.* In some cases, a defence is built into the legislation being examined, but very often is not. In addition, in common law jurisdictions there may be a concurrent common law defence sitting in the background which, again, is often missed by novice analysts. To a large extent the analysis of a defence is much like the consideration of the elements of an offence or cause of action. While the burden of establishing a valid defence rests with the party relying on it, there is an associated burden on the opponent to establish the defence is not available. In the criminal law this is linked to the burden and standard of proof, which we will examine later.

The way we now consider these elements ultimately depends on the extent to which these elements are contestable, either because the law is controversial, the evidence is controversial, or both. At this point you need to turn to the evidence in the specific case.

The role of evidence

Every crime leaves behind some evidence of its commission, although the extent to which that evidence is known, available or admissible will vary depending on the case. It is important to note that the longer it takes for a matter to come before a court, the weaker the evidence becomes. Physical evidence can be lost or destroyed, memory fades and becomes distorted through interpretation, and witnesses move around.[5] The qualitative aspects of the evidence available needs to be clear in the mind of the analyst. Here it is useful to consider what 'evidence' is. Again, in *HML v The Queen,* Gleeson CJ stated simply that 'Evidence is information which, according to certain governing general principles and more detailed rules, will be received by a court for the purpose of deciding issues of fact that arise for its decision'.[6] So, what you are looking for is information that will assist in both satisfying the elements you have already identified, as well as information that will serve to enliven *further* legal issues beyond the ones you initially identified.

As you will see, the sources of evidence are numerous and potentially extensive. Criminal prosecution briefs can be highly complex and voluminous. Ironically, in legal

5 The rules of evidence strongly assist here. Evidence may be held inadmissible or irrelevant on account of age or the absence of witnesses, for example. In addition, even when evidence is admitted, courts will often give warnings as to the reliability of certain types of evidence or may impose limits on the uses of evidence before the court.

6 *HML v The Queen* (2008) 245 ALR 204, 207 [4].

education it is more common for students to be provided with a very brief set of 'facts', which is often inadequate to engage with the complexities of the law.

This information now gives us a context in which to consider the law and the elements of it that we have initially identified. It moves us towards finding the law and elements that we have not identified that emerge out of the facts. The problem we face is that there is a lot more information here, but not all of it has legal significance, and there is also information here that may or may not be able to establish the case. We will return to a detailed examination of this problem later in the book. Before we begin to evaluate the evidence, we need to understand something more about the nature of fact finding in the criminal law.

Legal reasoning normally involves nuanced analysis of information from different sources, depending on the purpose of the analysis. It has empirical foundations in most cases but can also involve adverting to ethical and metaphysical components; even then, there is a tendency for legal thinkers to refer to and draw on established bodies of knowledge. In legal philosophy, for example, the evidence base tends to be from established 'positivist' thinkers in the field, such as HLA Hart,[7] Habermas[8] and Austin.[9] In the context of applied law, reasoning will involve the assessment and conditional relationship between law and fact, both of which are constituted in objectively observable information. Once the purpose of legal reasoning moves beyond theory into application, the role of evidence becomes crucial.

Evidence is essential to the application of law

In the context of criminal liability, evidence is fundamental to establishing both liability and culpability. Here evidence can be used both to establish the category of offence open on the facts and to determine the culpability of the offender and associated sentencing range for an offence of that kind. That is, the available evidence assists in evaluating whether the elements of the charge have been (or are likely to be) made out, and in determining a proportionate punishment. But, as we already observed, the evidence can also be used to disrupt the assumption of process, linked to the admissibility of evidence and the regularity of investigation procedure, as well as the existence or non-existence of a defence. Consequently, it is useful to think about evidence as falling under four different but intersecting headings: (1) elements of the offence, (2) culpability, (3) procedures and (4) defences.

It is important when thinking through a problem to be mindful of the empirical basis of law in the evidence available – this will be relevant both to establish guilt and determine an appropriate sentence. Both dimensions operate concurrently, although it is important not to merge the two analytically. You cannot, for example, charge a person with a circumstance of aggravation in a criminal charge as an element of the offence and rely on that as a sentencing factor.[10]

7 Herbert Hart, *The Concept of Law* (Oxford University Press, 3rd ed, 2012 [1961]).
8 Jurgen Habermas, *Between Facts and Norms*, tr William Rehg (Polity Press, 1996).
9 John Austin, *The Province of Jurisprudence Determined*, ed Wilfred Rumble (Cambridge University Press, 1995).
10 See, eg, *Crimes (Sentencing Procedure) Act 1999* (NSW) s 21A(2): 'The court is not to have regard to any such aggravating factor in sentencing if it is an element of the offence.'

Figure 2.1 The empirical foundations of legal reasoning

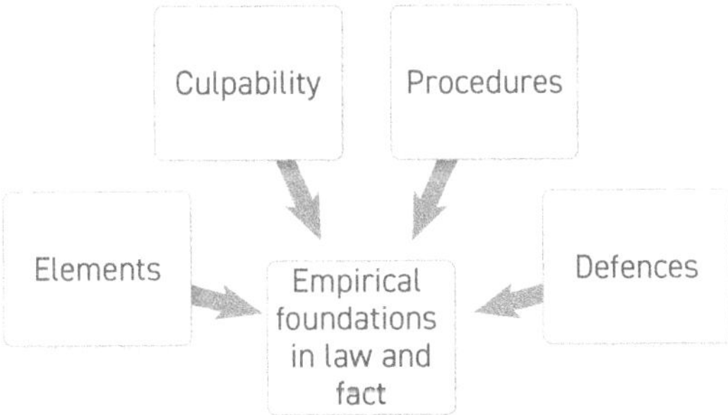

Evidence performs several functions:

(1) It directs attention to the nature of the charge(s).
(2) It assists in evaluating culpability and/or circumstances of aggravation.
(3) It directs attention to the existence of defences and/or circumstances in mitigation.
(4) It enlivens a consideration of the weight and admissibility of the evidence.
(5) It directs attention to the processes involved in the case that have legal consequence.
(6) It assists in identifying the availability of a defence.

In introductory criminal law courses, it is common for the laws of evidence to be excised or minimised for the purposes of incremental learning – but the student *must* remember that criminal law (including sentencing), procedural law and evidence law are part of a whole. Regrettably, it is common in legal education for criminal law to be placed in the first or second year of a course, mainly because it is 'interesting', when in fact it is one of the more complex areas of law because of the intersections of substantive and procedural criminal law, evidence, and sentencing.

The elements of the offence

Criminal law practice requires a process of accurate identification, interpretation and evaluation of evidence relating to the elements of the offence. The expression 'elements' refers to the relevant legal concepts that form a part of the matrix of reasoning necessary to determine the ultimate question of the guilt of the accused. Basically, what must be proven as points of proof. It includes the *operative concepts* within the words of the statute creating the offence, as well as the *ancillary concepts* existing outside but necessarily linked to the case through operation of law or the facts of the case.

Let's consider the case of Reggie Blade, who is 12 years old. He steals a CD entitled *Wagner's Greatest Hits* from a music shop.[11] He is caught and charged with larceny. In

11 We can assume that Reggie either has no idea what he has stolen or is a young man of refined tastes!

New South Wales, larceny is a common law offence, with the sentence limited by s 117 of the *Crimes Act*. Here the elements of the offence are sourced mainly in the common law, read in conjunction with the *Crimes Act*. The student must sufficiently characterise the elements of the offence sourced in the common law and the *Crimes Act*. The task requires identification of the elements of the offence, which in this case are sourced in case authorities. What are the elements of the offence?

The elements of an offence and the link with common law was considered by Gleeson CJ in *HML v The Queen*:

> In a criminal trial of an indictable offence, the indictment identifies the alleged offence. The prosecution sets out to prove the elements of the offence, that is to say, the specific offence alleged to have been committed by the accused. The jury will be directed, as a matter of law, that for a verdict of guilty it is necessary to be satisfied beyond reasonable doubt of those elements. *The elements of the offence, to the extent to which they are disputed, identify the facts in issue, which may be refined by particulars.* Depending upon the way in which the prosecution seeks to prove its case, or the way in which the defence is conducted, it may appear, as a matter of fact, that an element of the offence charged will not be established beyond reasonable doubt unless some subsidiary fact, relevant to a fact in issue, is proved to that standard. However, the legal requirement as to onus and standard of proof is related to the elements of the offence charged. In some cases, there may be only one available path to a conclusion of guilt, but often that is not so. Jurors are commonly instructed that they may be selective in their approach to the evidence, and even in their approach to different parts of the evidence of the one witness.[12]

Hence the elements of the offence are identified mainly through a consideration of three aspects of the problem.

First, there are the elements of the offence charged. This is based on the *words of the statute*, or the words of a concept located in the common law.[13] Typically, this will involve a combination of *physical element(s)*, *fault element(s)* and *qualifying or procedural elements*. Here the accurate identification of the elements is linked to the source of law. If the primary source of law is legislation, then these elements are located in the legislation relating to the charge(s) the person is alleged to have committed, or through characterisation of principle(s) in interpreting case authority(ies). If the source of law is the common law, then the relevant source is those cases that declare and modify the principle within the network of authorities. In some situations, there will be an overlap, where legislation may modify one or more of the common law components or, in some cases, abolish them.

12 (2008) 235 CLR 334, 350–1 [4] (emphasis added).

13 Note that this principle applies in common law jurisdictions only. In *Criminal Code* ('Code') jurisdictions, the Code is the primary source of law, although there may be associated cases confirming the interpretation of the Code. In many cases there will be a strong concurrence between the common law and the Code, but much depends on the exact wording of the Code.

Second, there are the *elements in the surrounding legalities.* This is determined by the source of law that governs the concept under consideration. Depending on the issue(s), these legalities may be numerous, or none. In the context of the criminal law, such matters typically include: (1) procedural rules relating to the authorisation of investigation (eg the existence or legality of a warrant); (2) overlapping rules linked to the specific qualities of the accused (eg aspects of law relating to the accused that are not part of the elements of the offence (such as doli incapax)); and (3) overlapping rules linked to the law affecting the accused (eg constitutional questions; administrative law).

Third, there are the *issues in the evidence.* Here we are really talking about the available evidence that can satisfy the legal elements needed to make out the offence. However, the very nature of this evidence is that it can have its own legal dimensions (eg matters relevant to the culpability of the accused), as well as enlivening the rules of evidence (eg hearsay or tendency evidence). The evidence may point towards matters relevant to the sentencing of the accused, as well as matters that may trigger particular rules of evidence.

For the purposes of an introductory criminal law course, your main focus is usually on the first aspect. However, keep in mind that the criminal law is part of a larger network of law and fact that has an influence on the determination of guilt. Simply stated, an introductory criminal law course is woefully inadequate preparation for deep-level analysis of evidence and criminal litigation. Learning the basics is important but being able to integrate new learning is of equal importance.

Returning to the example of Reggie Blade's culpability, the elements of the substantive offence are stipulated in the common law in the leading Australian authority, *Ilich v R* (1986) 162 CLR 110. In that case Wilson and Dawson JJ stated:

> At common law, larceny is committed by a person who, without the consent of the owner, fraudulently and without a claim of right made in good faith, takes and carries away anything capable of being stolen with intent, at the time of such taking, permanently to deprive the owner thereof ... Because larceny at common law requires a trespass – it is sometimes described as an offence against possession – a person lawfully in possession of something cannot be guilty of larceny of it.[14]

At this point there are two comments to be made. The first is that the quote gives us the common law elements. The second is that there is an underlying and hidden dimension at play that you will only become aware of with research and background reading. The underlying dimension is the context of the law – in this regard most jurisdictions in Australia have followed the English evolution of abolishing the common law and replacing it with provisions based on the *Theft Act 1968* (UK). The other dimension is an anachronism, which is that larceny was historically a felony that could result in the death penalty – this is why the common law has so many elements. This

14 At 123.

hidden dimension of the task is not presently important, as our task is concerned with ascertaining the elements of the offence. However, being aware of the jurisdictional differences is useful and, depending on the purpose, may be relevant in a broader discussion.

At common law liability is determined by classifying and evaluating the elements of the offence as a division between physical and fault elements: actus reus and mens rea. Unpacking the elements would look like this:

> *At common law, larceny is committed* **[this is the conclusion]** *by a person* **[legal personality]** *who, without the consent of the owner* **[physical element]**, *fraudulently* **[mental element]** *and without a claim of right made in good faith* **[defence]**, *takes and carries away* **[physical element]** *capable of being stolen* **[physical element]** *with intent, at the time of such taking, permanently to deprive the owner thereof* **[mental element]** ... *Because larceny at common law requires a trespass – it is sometimes described as an offence against possession – a person lawfully in possession of something cannot be guilty of larceny of it.*

From this we can determine our elements as shown in Table 2.1.

Table 2.1 The physical and mental elements of an offence

Physical elements (actus reus)	**Mental elements (mens rea)**
• The physical seizing of property	• The taking was fraudulent/dishonest
• Without consent of the person in possession	• The intention of the taking was to permanently deprive the owner of the property
• The property was capable of being stolen	
Defence The taking was without claim of right	

The hidden law in the elements

It is tempting, and convenient, to simply stop at this point. It is a common error of novices to simply conduct a 'surface' reading of the law, identify the elements and then make simple declarations that because certain evidence is present there is necessarily proof of the element. That is a dangerous assumption. The older a legal principle is, the more likely there will be consideration of those elements in decided cases. Most of these will be simple applications of the law, but some will involve interpretation and shape new meaning, which extends the meaning of one or more of the elements. Larceny, for example, has been around for centuries, and as such there are numerous cases on each element, with the result that a thorough consideration of the elements may involve extended analysis and research going beyond the simple identification of the elements. Accordingly, the first phase of the analysis involves identifying the elements and how these are subsequently characterised and defined.

The second aspect involves thinking about the hidden intersections that are less clear. This part relies on having a broad understanding of the law. Some of intersections *will* apply in all cases, but most are *conditional* on the existence of certain conditions in law and/or fact. An example of what *will* apply in all cases are the specific procedural rules linked to the disposal of the charge. An example of *conditional* law that may apply are *admissibility rules*. In the case of Reggie Blade there are at least two hidden intersections: (1) the law linked to the procedure and (2) the law linked to the age of the offender.

In New South Wales, larceny is an indictable offence. However, it is an offence that is dealt with summarily in a Local Court unless an election is made to proceed to trial. The party who may elect is determined by the value of the property.[15] This aspect imports a degree of complexity, as it involves exploring a different body of law, and paying attention to the facts. Not only is this relevant to the procedure, but it also has an effect on the penalty. Larceny has a maximum penalty of five years' imprisonment, but if the matter is determined in the Local Court, then the maximum penalty is two years, or a fine capped at 20 to 50 penalty units. Now there is *another* intersection. What is a 'penalty unit'? A penalty unit is an abstract value that enables Parliament to uniformly adjust the value of a fine without having to pass legislation across the entire spectrum of law. In New South Wales, a penalty unit is set by s 17 of the *Criminal Procedure Act 1986* (NSW) at $110. The penalty unit discussion takes place in the context of a larger overlapping area of law linked to sentencing, which in itself is a vast field of law grounded in the common law, as well as in legislation.

In New South Wales, the age of criminal responsibility begins at 10, with a common law rebuttable presumption that a person between 10 and 14 years of age is doli incapax.[16] This body of law is 'conditional', in the sense that it only applies to your reasoning when the facts trigger its use. In our scenario, the offender is 12 years old, which means that doli incapax is a necessary consideration. Consequently, a thorough analysis of the problem would require examination of that. But in addition, the age of the offender also has procedural implications, as the matter would necessarily have to be determined in the Children's Court.

As can be seen, even in a simple hypothetical there are often significant complexities. A thorough examination would look something like the process shown in Figure 2.2.

15 *Criminal Procedure Act 1986* (NSW) ss 260, 267, 268, sch 1 pt 2 cl 3(a).
16 *Children (Criminal Proceedings) Act 1987* (NSW) s 5; *RP v The Queen* (2016) 259 CLR 641.

Figure 2.2 Factors in thinking through larceny at common law

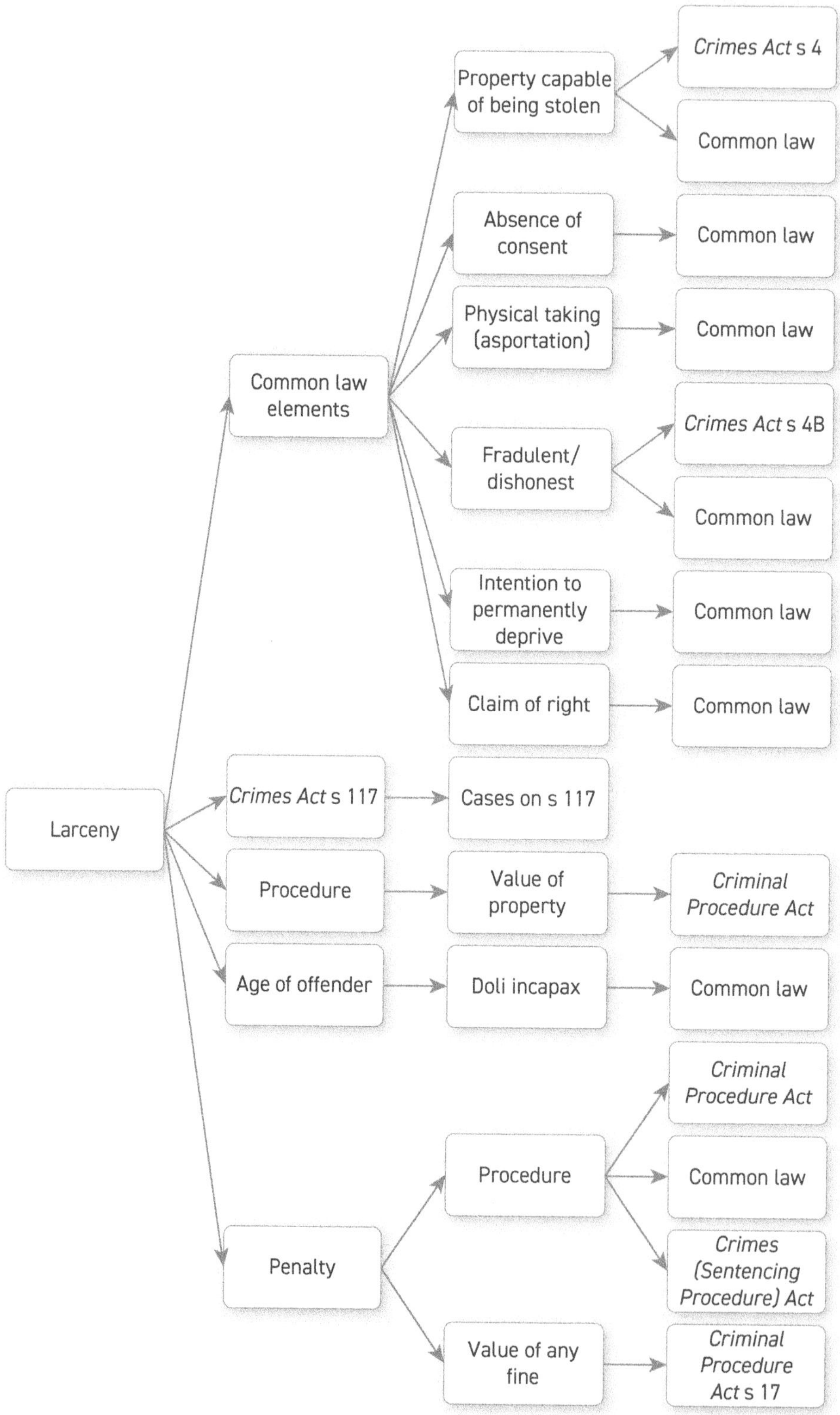

Key points

- The central purpose of problem solving is to predict as accurately as possible the outcome of a scenario should the matter proceed to court.
- The task is concerned with the identification of the relevant rules and their combination with other rules.
- Your task then turns to proper interpretation of those rules, drawing on the relevant definitions, meaning and qualified interpretation where case principles and the rules of statutory interpretation apply.
- The extent to which you engage in an analysis of those terms depends on the problem at hand.
- Being able to identify and consider the hidden legalities comes from reading broadly.

3 FACT FINDING

Using evidence principles to think about facts

Law students routinely forget that the legal tradition has been concerned with fact finding for centuries. Evidence law is grounded in specific principles, which translate into specific rules applied on a case-by-case basis. Such rules include rules concerned with the reliability of evidence, procedural fairness and the power of courts to exclude evidence. Of these there are two of present importance which must inform your appraisal of a case. First, the evidence accepted by a court must be legally admissible. Second, the evidence presented to the court must be sufficiently *reliable* so that the tribunal of fact[1] is able to draw conclusions about whether or not an alleged fact existed in circumstances where the tribunal of fact has not witnessed the event for itself. Legal reasoning is empirically grounded and draws upon centuries of human experience in the examination of materials of this kind, recorded in thousands of cases. With that in mind, principles from evidence law can be used to help us to think about facts as part of the analysis of a legal problem. Indeed, turning your mind to the rich body of evidence law is essential. It is not possible in a book like this to engage with evidence law in any detail. Evidence law in Australia is comprehensively examined by several authoritative authors, to which the reader is referred to for detail.[2] However, for present purposes we will consider a range of important and fundamental principles that can be used for preliminary examination and analysis of information.

Elements in law

The fundamental importance of the elements in law to legal problem solving was noted in Chapter 2. Law is characterised by the presence, in text, of statements that contain core concepts, with legal meaning – these concepts are essential to mobilising a particular rule or cluster of them. Accurate identification and characterisation of the relevant elements is critical because, without their identification, your subsequent analysis of facts will be

1 The tribunal of fact makes decisions on the facts of a case based on the presentation of evidence to the court. In cases in which a jury is empaneled (usual in indictable criminal cases), the jury is the tribunal of fact. In the lower courts, and in indictable cases in which there is an election to proceed without a jury, the judge (or magistrate) is the tribunal of fact.

2 John Dyson Heydon, *Cross on Evidence* (Lexis Nexis, 12th ed, 2020); John Anderson, *Uniform Evidence Law: Text and Essential Cases* (Federation Press, 4th ed, 2021); Stephen Odgers, *Uniform Evidence Law* (Lawbook Co, 16th ed, 2021); Neil Williams et al, *Uniform Evidence in Australia* (LexisNexis Butterworths, 2nd ed, 2020); Andrew Ligertwood and Gary Edmond, *Australian Evidence: A Principled Approach to the Common Law and Uniform Acts* (LexisNexis Butterworths, 6th ed, 2018).

devoid of purpose. Facts have meaning only in relationship with the rule being considered. As discussed above, identifying the elements is essential because it is only with reference to the elements of the cause of action, relief, remedy, or rule structure that the subsequent analysis of the facts can take place. In the criminal law, questions of liability are directly linked to either the elements of an offence – that is, what the prosecution must prove beyond reasonable doubt in order to convict the accused – or to the elements of a defence. These considerations may intersect with procedural law, such as in relation to the validity of a warrant. In private law, the elements of law will often be determined by the parties themselves in the terms of agreement or associated governing statue. Things are slightly different when it comes to constitutional law, because the components of a dispute linked to the *Australian Constitution* are entrenched within the words of the constitutional instrument, as well as within the complex variety of cases that determine the scope and ambit of constitutional principles. But the point is that any consideration of facts and evidence must be undertaken by reference to specific elements within the relevant body of law.

Facts in issue

Litigated matters normally involve some dispute between the parties over the interpretation of law, or the ascertainment of facts that have legal consequences. Matters in issue can be surprisingly complicated, including 'main facts', multiple issues and mixed questions of law and fact, as well as subordinate and collateral facts. This is often very confusing. For our purposes, we will limit the discussion to the essential facts in issue. In *Cross on Evidence*, John Dyson Heydon wrote:

> The main facts in issue are all those facts which the plaintiff (or applicant or petitioner) in a civil action, or the prosecutor in criminal proceedings, must prove in order to succeed, together with any further facts that the defendant (or respondent) or accused must prove in order to establish a defence. The main facts in issue in a particular case can only be ascertained by reference to the substantive law and any procedure which defines the issues, for example, pleadings.[3]

It is assumed that all elements in a cause of action are in issue unless and until the parties agree on the existence of certain facts. It is open to the parties to agree on some or all of the facts that establish legal categories on which the court can make decisions. Basically, the facts in issue in a case are those elements in law that need to be proven by the relevant party to the relevant standard, where those elements are contested by the opponent. As the courts in the common law tradition rely on the parties to present their case, the parties are at liberty to agree on some or all of the facts. With the rise of proactive case management, the parties are required to restrict their argument in court to those matters that are not agreed to and to agree on matters that are not contested. In a criminal case the prosecution, as discussed in Chapter 2, always has the burden of proof in that it needs to prove the elements of an offence beyond reasonable doubt in order to convict the accused. What that means is that the elements of an offence are always in issue as a starting proposition.

3 John Dyson Heydon, *Cross on Evidence* (Lexis Nexis, 11th ed, 2017) 13 [1080].

Modern case management approaches to the criminal law tend to encourage the parties to agree on certain facts that are not contested, and to try and sharply focus upon those matters that are in contest and necessary to prove. For example, in a sexual assault case there may be forensic evidence that clearly establishes that sexual intercourse took place. In that case the accused may admit that fact, taking it out of dispute as an agreed fact. The issue in dispute may be the question of consent, which becomes the live issue in the trial. The basic point is that facts may or may not be in dispute, depending on agreement or concessions by the parties. Where there is no agreement, then all of the facts need to be proven to the relevant standard by the party that has the burden of proof.[4]

Problem-solving hint

When undertaking a problem-solving assignment, it is important to read the instructions of any hypothetical that has been presented to you. If the hypothetical advises that one or more set of facts have been agreed to, then it is important to recognise that they have been agreed to, and not to spend too much time on analysing that aspect of the problem. If there is no indication that facts are agreed to, then you should not assume anything, and spend time addressing the relevant elements appropriately.

Scepticism

A useful starting point is assuming there is no evidence supporting an allegation. Simply stated, be sceptical from the outset. Scepticism is a branch of philosophy and jurisprudence. Legal theory is rarely taught in the early years at law school, and it is often the case that students are 'taught' basic legal problem solving before they even hear about the concept of scepticism. This is not a book about jurisprudence, so the reader is referred to those authors if interested in the detail. For present purposes, scepticism may be understood as an analytical tool used to test assertions of knowledge. At its simplest, scepticism invites a suspension of belief until evidence is presented and tested. A belief is a conclusion linked to a willingness to accept that an assertion of truth is correct.

From a legal point of view, that is problematic – especially where the assertion is that person X has committed a crime, because the belief engages a process whereby the power of the state to punish that person is legitimised. This position simply invites us to make two assumptions intended to protect the person:

(1) There is no law on X.
(2) There are no facts supporting X.

4 This is an advanced concept, complicated further by the fact there are exceptions to the burden of proof. For example, in the context of mental illness there is a common law (and statutory) legal burden of proof on the accused to establish the condition on the balance of probabilities, which the prosecution must then disprove beyond reasonable doubt. See, eg, *M'Naughten's Case* (1843) 8 ER 718; *R v Falconer* (1990) 171 CLR 30; *Mental Health and Cognitive Impairment Forensic Provisions Act 2020* (NSW) s 28.

This position requires the analyst to now embark on the task of establishing the empirical foundations of both questions. What is the law on X? Are there facts that support X? This position is easiest to engage in when you have some idea about the relevant rule system being deployed. An example is where the accused has been charged with a particular offence and the elements of that offence are known. It is a serious thing to make an accusation with coercive legal consequence, particularly of a crime, and as such you should assume there is no evidence supporting the allegation. That is, the element does not exist.

Yet even where there is some evidence that a fact exists, legal scepticism invites deeper consideration. Just because there is *some* evidence does not mean it can satisfy the relevant standard of proof, or that there is not some difference in explanation consistent with innocence. For example, let's assume that the driver of a vehicle crashed into the rear of a car at a set of traffic lights. The passenger of the vehicle is killed, while the driver is seriously injured. On examination of the vehicle, police found two empty bottles of beer in the footwell of the passenger's seat. What uses might be made of that evidence? One possibility is the conclusion that the driver of the vehicle was intoxicated at the time of the event. If the driver was charged with dangerous driving causing death, the fact of intoxication could become an aggravating factor in the charge. But what other possibilities are there? There are many. The passenger could have been drinking. The bottles may simply be rubbish yet to be thrown out. Even if the driver had consumed the contents, two bottles of beer would be unlikely to render the driver 'intoxicated'. Without fact scepticism assertions of fact can easily become accepted and sometimes dangerous narratives.

Fact scepticism can also be applied to gaps in evidence. The law, for example, may require evidence of one or more elements that are not apparently present on the evidence for facts that you are working with. You should not assume that just because it's missing that it does not exist. In practical terms, it could mean that the process of evidence gathering is incomplete, and that is something that needs to be considered in any advice that you subsequently give. In the sexual assault scenario above, there is a live issue as to consent. There may be no evidence of explicit consent, or a contested version of events. A party may be lying. The most difficult cases are those where there is physical evidence that is missing. Murder cases, for example, will sometimes involve an allegation that a person has killed another and disposed of the body.

A final note on fact scepticism is to aim to keep an open mind. It is easy to shift from scepticism to nihilism. Prosecutors, in particular, can easily become convinced that a person accused of a crime is guilty of it, blinded by the assumption that a missing piece of evidence must exist in cases where it does not, or that the person has committed a lesser offence to the one charged.

Relevance

Probably the most important threshold rule in the analysis of evidence is *relevance*. Relevance is the threshold test for evidence in law. If a piece of evidence is relevant to a fact in issue, then it needs to be considered to a greater or lesser extent as part of your reasoning. Indeed, if the evidence is relevant, it is admissible unless it is excluded by some other rule.[5] As we

5 This is true at common law and under uniform evidence law. See *Evidence Act 1995* (NSW) ss 55–6.

will see later, that also includes things that are not evident or clear in the factual problem. This rule is equally applicable to questions of law. Is the law also relevant? That is, is the identified law capable of being applied in the fact/law matrix?

As a matter of law, *a piece of evidence is relevant if it could rationally affect the probability of the existence or non-existence of a fact in issue.*[6] There is no requirement that a piece of evidence be conclusive on any point; it is sufficient so long as there is a minimal logical and probative connection between the fact in issue and the evidence presented. Some cases depend on the presence of a small number of highly probative pieces of evidence, while other cases depend on a constellation of related but minor pieces of evidence that in themselves are insufficient to establish a fact, but in combination leave no other conclusion but an overwhelming one.

The same rule of relevance can be applied in cases where there are doubts about the appropriate law that can be applied to the problem: can the rule of law rationally be applied in this particular case? Sometimes you will be unsure as to whether or not the rule being considered is correct. When in doubt, apply the rule to the fact matrix to test your thinking. If the rule has plausible application, then it is relevant to consider it. If the application is clearly wrong, or absurd, it may be ignored or discounted.

Admissibility issues

Part of the function of the laws of evidence is to act as a filter for the court in relation to evidence that is either contrary to public policy or has been obtained in such a way that its reliability is in doubt, and is excluded, either by a mandatory rule or in the exercise of judicial discretion. Part of the analysis you will need to undertake is not only concerned with spotting the evidence capable of supporting the cause of action, but also considering whether that piece of information may be qualified or excluded through the operation of the laws of evidence. This is something that can only be undertaken when you have a broad command of the law, rather than knowledge of a discrete subject area. For present purposes we will note that questions of admissibility are something that need to be considered, but we will move on at this point, and return to questions of admissibility when we are looking at advanced problem solving in a later chapter. As mentioned at the outset, there is a disconnect between criminal law and evidence in legal education as the subjects are taught separately, and often some years apart.

Weight of evidence

Part of your analysis will need to consider the nature of the evidence itself, and its persuasive power. Sometimes this can easily be done by setting out the evidence in a chart and assigning a numerical value of 1 to 10 against each piece of evidence, where 10 is a compelling and unarguable fact, and 1 is so minor it barely passes the threshold for relevant probative value. This is sometimes referred to as *weight* of evidence – a conceptual measure going to the satisfaction in the mind of the tribunal of fact as to the extent to which that piece of evidence supports the conclusion that the element exists. For present purposes our concern is to ask a simple question. That question is how convinced would a court be by

6 Ibid s 55.

this piece of evidence in its relationship with the facts in issue? As mentioned earlier, some pieces of evidence are simply so convincing that virtually nothing else is required to support the fact in issue, and sometimes the entire case. Conversely, sometimes a piece of evidence is plausibly connected to the fact in issue, but of itself adds little to the overall case. Such matters are not necessarily to be ignored, however, because in combination multiple pieces of evidence can support an irresistible conclusion or inference based on the relationship between the accused and a multitude of minor but sufficient pieces of evidence.

Questions relevant to the persuasive power of evidence will vary according to the *type* of evidence, the *source* of the evidence, and its *proximity* to the offence. In some cases, a piece of evidence will be physical and directly connected to the offence. For example, let's say that a person was stabbed. They were found in the kitchen by ambulance officers. A large knife was retrieved from the same room, covered in the victim's blood. That piece of evidence is irresistible in supporting the conclusion that the victim was stabbed with that knife. There is no other rational conclusion. If the knife *also* had the fingerprints of the accused on the handle, there is a strong inference the accused stabbed the victim.

In some cases, the evidence will be something that a person has seen, or heard, and they are subsequently required to give a statement to the police, and later testimony in a court. What a person saw and perceived may be highly probative, but at the same time it may not be. For example, let's say that a person saw a fight on a crowded street late at night, with many people moving around, and poor lighting. In that case the best evidence that a witness can give may simply be that they observed a fight involving several people. Whether they are able to identify anyone is another question. Fact scepticism allows us to identify conceptual pressure points in evidence useful for cross-examination and in evaluating the strength of a case. The point here is that you are invited to always consider the persuasive power of the evidence that you are working with and take into account the extent to which that piece of evidence is linked to the elements of the law being applied, and the extent to which that piece of evidence satisfies the persuasive burden that a particular fact exists or not. This can be surprisingly challenging in cases where there is in fact no evidence of a particular fact in issue. You will still need to make an assessment about the importance of a particular element, and the significance of the absence of evidence related to it. The absence of a critical element in a course of action may in fact be fatal to pursuing the matter at all. At the very least, you would be called on to advise the client, or advise the marker of an examination, of the absence of an important piece of information, and evaluate the significance of it, and what would happen if no evidence on that point was forthcoming.

Hint on the value of evidence

There are two useful clues on the value of evidence. The first is to ask yourself whether a piece of evidence relates to a *critical* element in the law. A critical element is usually unique to the action, the absence of which means there is a cause of action of that kind. For example, death is an essential element for a charge of murder. Similarly, if a person was being charged with causing a grievous injury, proving the injury is 'grievous' is essential. Where an essential element is missing, alternatives must be considered.

The second clue is linked to litigation. One of the pressure points that can be identified in litigation is how strongly the opposition protects and argues for the existence, or the acceptance, of a specific piece of evidence. These are routinely connected to critical elements in a cause of action. For example, in a case involving dangerous driving causing death, the evidence of a blood sample establishing a high level of intoxication would be strongly protected by the prosecution because it is a critical element.

Sources of evidence

Hypothetical problems used in legal education are often based upon the same kinds of information and sources of evidence that exist in the 'real' world. Ideally, a good hypothetical problem will be as realistic and close to practice as possible. Discussions about the Frog Prince and the promise of a princess to marry him are, simply put, rather childish and unnecessary in professional legal education. A decent problem question will involve a range of parties, sources and events that are grounded in the realm of human experience and possibility. With that in mind, the type of evidence that you will be looking at in an authentic hypothetical will in most cases be similar to the sources of evidence that you would normally encounter.

There are four main sources of evidence. The first is the *oral testimony* of witnesses. Testimony is a verbal report to the court, based upon what the person has seen, perceived, understood and in many cases interpreted of events that have taken place within the field of perception. The witness may have been directly affected by some event or action, or may be an onlooker, or someone who has been told about some aspect of the event. The second is *physical evidence,* which relates to the physical traces and artefacts linked to the event. This can include images, sounds and recordings that capture some aspect of the event. The third common source of evidence is evidence found in *documents*. This category overlaps with physical evidence, but also has some unique aspects. Documents often comprise an archive that contains descriptions and reports of what a person observed. When the document is being used as truth of what is represented in the document, this is known in evidence law as a 'hearsay purpose' and may be inadmissible. However, there are many exceptions to the hearsay rule where documents are concerned. As you progress in your study of law, you will discover that a good deal of law is wrapped around the use and concept of hearsay evidence. The final, common form of evidence is the *report of an expert* on some aspect of the case. These four sources of evidence are not the only ones, but they are the most common, both in practice and in assessment tasks. We will now look at testimonial evidence in more detail.

Oral testimony

When we talk about 'oral testimony', we are talking about what a person reports to a court, under oath or affirmation, when they are being questioned by the court. Such evidence is adduced through the process of initially soliciting a statement in the person's own words that is an accurate report of events based on recollection. This is then subject to critical questioning in the form of cross-examination for the purpose of testing the reliability of the evidence. Such evidence is highly regarded by the court because it provides a narrative of what the person has perceived and allows the court to evaluate the truthfulness of the witness, and assess memory and the distortions of perception.

There is often a disconnect between what a person says on the day in court, what they report they have seen and experienced at an earlier time, and what they perceived and experienced at the time of the event. Over time, the accuracy of recollection can fade and become distorted. Memory can also be indelible, so while the specifics of certain aspects of an event may vanish with time, the core substance of recollection may last a lifetime. That observation is consistent with ordinary human experience, but also the psychology of memory. For this reason, it is unwise to assume that just because something happened years in the past, that recollection of it is necessarily flawed, or conversely that something freshly observed is necessarily accurate. The function of evidence in chief and cross-examination is to test the reliability of the recollection and the witness.

Practically speaking, what most lawyers have access to are transcripts of interviews, as well as statements made by complainants and witnesses. In the context of problem-based assessments, the complexity of that material will vary, ranging from simple descriptions in a hypothetical (as in Appendix A) through to more advanced documents that directly replicate affidavits, witness statements and police reports. The essential point is that those statements will rarely capture the full narrative. This is why skilled interviewing is so important, including taking time to speak to witnesses and complainants in some detail before a case gets to court. It will not only enable you to fill any gaps in the reported material, but also help you identify them and anticipate their likely effect when the person eventually gives that evidence in court. In the context of problem-based assignments, that process is not usually available, but there is no reason in principle why you cannot identify aspects of evidence that may be problematic and require clarification where relevant to do so.

The extent to which hypothetical problems provide a complete picture will vary according to the available detail. Most problem scenarios will be patchy, although some major tasks will draw on a lot of detail and may include an array of written statements made by fictional characters. At this point it is useful to reflect on the way in which statements are used in practice. As a general proposition, out-of-court statements are inadmissible unless they fall under some exception, such as an admission. In civil cases it is very common for statements to be made by way of affidavits,[7] which have the function of being considered oral testimony in written form; the deponent may be cross-examined, or the document accepted as evidence of its contents. In criminal cases previous statements are generally not admissible where the deponent gives oral evidence unless the maker of the statement is not available or there is a prior inconsistent statement.[8] Hypotheticals will often diverge from what would normally be the case in practice, but in more advanced analysis may require a consideration of calling certain witnesses as part of the answer.

7 See, eg, *Uniform Civil Procedure Rules 2005* (NSW) r 31.1.
8 See, eg, *Evidence Act 1995* (NSW) s 65.

Those issues aside, it is now worth thinking further about the nature of oral evidence. This may be understood as consisting of distinct *categories of reporting*.

Direct experience

The first common category of reporting is based on direct experience. The person has experienced an event directly through the senses. In the context of the criminal law, that is usually some kind of prohibited conduct, circumstance or result engineered by the offender(s), experienced by the witness to a greater or lesser extent. The experience of injury and harm is usually linked to the desire to report, retaliate or flee. Reporting is typically linked to a desire for the offender(s) to be brought before a court and punished for the wrong but can equally be linked to the marshalling of allies for the purpose of retaliation, and for the comfort and protection that comes with having allies. Here we are concerned with the report of a person who was directly injured or affected by the offending behaviour, or sufficiently proximate to it to have direct experience of it. In this context that experience may be before, during or after the event. This kind of evidence is critical, because it usually forms the crux of the complaint to authorities.

Skilled counsel will be wary of the distinctions between inviting a witness to report their experiences to the court, giving an interpretation of it or speculating about some part of it outside their perception. For example, in a case where the offender struck the victim across the face, it is one thing to give evidence of being hit by the accused, and quite another to ask whether the person intended to hit the victim. The former is a report of experience; the latter is an opinion. Problem-based assessments often lack this kind of high-level detail, but at the very least the student can learn an important lesson in knowing the difference between information clearly presented in the brief and speculating. Students should avoid speculating and drawing conclusions about matters not present in the brief, or otherwise not reasonably open as inferences. While inferences can be made, there are specific rules linked to inferential reasoning (discussed below).

Indirect experience

This category is concerned with onlookers, namely those that are present to directly observe the event but are not the subjects of the event. Evidence at this level is normally highly probative because the person often has the opportunity to see the larger picture. This kind of evidence often confirms and extends the perception of the direct subject, and when the testimony is aligned it essentially corroborates and gives the testimony greater weight in its believability. Witnesses who are not linked to the event apart from perceiving it are often able to give reliable evidence of considerable weight, provided there is clear opportunity for the relevant perception to take place. The assumption is that the witness has no reason to give evidence at all as they are otherwise unaffected by it. That is, however, an assumption to be made carefully. The witness may well have motive to be untruthful or biased in their assessment of the event. But the point here is to consider the availability of witnesses who are otherwise not directly involved as part of the analysis.

Hearsay

This category of evidence encompasses something that the witness has been told by someone else. The problem with this kind of evidence is the witness has not directly perceived it themselves. Their understanding of the event comes from another person. Such evidence is notoriously unreliable, but equally can be an important part of a web of evidence. Special rules apply to evidence of this kind. The starting point is that when this kind of evidence is used as proof of the fact contained in the evidence, it is used for a 'hearsay purpose'. Such evidence is inadmissible unless some exception applies. One such exception is where a person who directly perceived the event relates that event to another, which includes matters reported by the victim to others outside of court. Students of evidence will know that this kind of 'first-hand' hearsay[9] is an exception to the hearsay rule, and as such is admissible in a court in some jurisdictions. A classic example of this is where the witness gives evidence initially to police in the form of an oral statement, which they then repeat in court. The police officer may also give evidence that they were told of certain experiences by the witness, to the effect that 'Person X told me …'. This is to be contrasted with 'second-hand' hearsay. In that context the witness receives a report from another that someone else told them (A → B → C). B says to you (C) that 'Person A told me …'. That kind of hearsay is inadmissible. What is required in those cases is that either person B or A is located to give evidence. This is not because what person A actually said is necessarily wrong or inaccurate, but because centuries of human experience have shown that when people pass on messages to one another there is a tendency for distortions to emerge which make the accuracy and reliability of this evidence problematic. It is also an important rule of procedural fairness that a person accused of a crime is entitled to have their accusers give evidence about what was actually perceived by them, and not what has been told to them by others.

Thinking about perception and reliability

What is common to all categories of testimonial evidence (except fantasy) is the fact that the evidence is perceived through the senses. Here it is useful to think about the nature of perception.

- What did the person see?
  - What were the conditions?
  - What was the lighting like?
  - How much time was involved between event A and B?
  - What opportunity(ies) did the person have to observe the event?
  - Did they recognise the offender(s)?
  - How clearly did they see the event and person/s involved?
- What did the person hear?
  - How clearly was it heard?
  - If it was something another person said, how clearly was it heard?
  - Did the person recognise the speaker?

9 Ibid s 62.

Fundamentally, the reason why we pay attention to the reporting of another is to assess two things: reliability and believability.

In some cases, the only available evidence will be a chain of pieces or fragments of evidence that point towards guilt, rather than direct evidence of it. These are known as 'circumstantial cases'. Common law has evolved rules that serve to both permit and control evidence based on circumstantial evidence, which allows the tribunal of fact to draw inferences from that evidence. In *R v Ryan*, for example, Mahoney JA outlined a process for this kind of reasoning in these terms:

> ... the question to be determined is whether, from the existence of Fact A, it should be inferred that ... Fact X existed, exists or will exist. There are two steps in this reasoning process: is it possible to draw that inference, and (if it is), should it be drawn in the particular case? In principle, it is possible to draw that inference that X did exist if human experience has shown that in a sufficient number of cases where A has been found to exist, X will have existed.
>
> If the inference is possible, it remains to be determined whether, in the circumstances of the particular case, it should be drawn. At the risk of over-refining common sense, this part of the reasoning may be described as follows. In some cases, the relationship between A and X is invariable and almost always so: whenever X exists, A will have existed. In such a case, the inference is not merely a possible one: it is proper that it be drawn in fact. But difficulties arise where the conjunction is less than invariable ...
>
> ... in my opinion, it helps in understanding the questions which have arisen in other cases, the way they have been answered, and what has been said in the course of answering them.
>
> If it be concluded that the inference is open, it remains for the jury to determine whether, in the circumstances, the inference should be drawn.[10]

At this point you need only be aware that once there are inferences being relied on by the prosecution, there are further (and quite complex rules) that you will go on to study in your Evidence subject in due course. For present purposes, it is enough to know a fundamental rule in relation to the extent to which you can rely on inferences as circumstantial evidence, known as the 'Hodge Test'. In *R v Hodge* (1838) 168 ER 1136, Baron Alderson held that guilt (in circumstantial cases based on inference) should not only be a rational inference but should be the *only* rational inference that could be drawn from the circumstances. This problem often arises in the case of murder where the victim's body is missing. In such cases there are numerous instances where the prosecution has succeeded based on circumstantial evidence, but the circumstances must be such that there is no other rational hypothesis other than the accused has killed the victim.[11]

The problem with this rule is that it is a rule of general application but is to be regarded only as a starting point. Much depends on the nature of the case and the evidence available. More recently, in *Edwards v The Queen*, Brennan J illustrated the problem with

10 *R v Ryan* (unreported, NSWCCA, 15 April 1994).
11 See, eg, *Azzopardi v The Queen* (2001) 205 CLR 50; *Weissenseiner v The Queen* (1993) 178 CLR 217.

inferences as being necessarily linked to the evidence from which the inferences may be drawn. In essence, when drawing an inference of guilt from the combination of facts, precise identification of the facts is required, and those facts must be established beyond reasonable doubt.[12] *Edwards* highlights the problem that in some cases the determination of guilt relies on the totality of a series of propositions going towards proof of guilt. Cases of this kind are exceedingly complex and most of the time will not be the kind of case encountered in undergraduate assessment. However, being aware of cases relying on this level of complexity is a useful learning experience.

The burden of proof

We began with the idea that law is an applied discipline. This is especially true of the criminal law because criminal conviction demands evidence to satisfy the decision maker that the accused is guilty of the alleged charge. The requirement to produce evidence to establish the fact is known as the *burden of proof*. This concept is made up of several sub-parts and is sometimes hard to understand. Opinions vary on the make-up of the 'burdens', but for present purposes we will consider three: the 'ultimate burden', the 'legal burden' and the 'evidential burden'.[13] Each of these arise at different points in time during a trial, and the analyst needs to be mindful of them.

The *ultimate burden* relates to the result. That is, the accused is either guilty or not. This is determined by considering the totality of evidence admitted at trial, in its relationship with the elements of the offence. The weight of evidence required for this conclusion is linked to the 'standard of proof'. In civil matters this is the balance of probabilities,[14] while in criminal cases it is beyond reasonable doubt.[15]

The *legal (or persuasive) burden* relates to the requirement to prove a particular issue during the trial. There will be multiple issues during a criminal trial, normally linked to the elements of the offence, that must be established in order for the ultimate burden to be discharged. In a criminal trial, the prosecution has the onus of proving the elements of the offence, and of disproving the existence of any defence raised by the accused or emerging out of the evidence. The accused may have a legal burden depending on specific rules arising.[16]

The *evidential burden* is linked to the legal burden and is the obligation to produce and present sufficient evidence on the issue that is asserted as fact by the party in the proceedings.[17] This burden arises wherever a party makes an assertion relevant to the case. Although this burden exists in relation to the elements of the offence, it also transcends it because many assertions in a case will not be linked to the elements of the offence. Rather, the evidence may be a counterclaim, such as an alibi, or contextual information relevant to circumstances of mitigation.

12 *Edwards v The Queen* (1993) 178 CLR 193, 202.
13 Opinions differ on categorisation. JB Thayer, writing in 1898, argued there were three uses of the term (outlined here), whereas John Dyson Heydon in *Cross on Evidence* recognised two and ignored the third.
14 See, eg, *Evidence Act 1995* (NSW) s 140.
15 See, eg, ibid s 141.
16 Heydon (n 3) 331.
17 Ibid 332.

In a criminal trial, the legal burden may be identified as those components of a case on which the judge gives directions to the jury in reaching a conclusion; whereas the evidential burden arises during the trial and determines whether or not the judge admits the evidence and leaves it as a component for the jury to determine. In this way 'the evidential burden governs what the Judge does',[18] and 'the persuasive burden governs what the Judge says, in directing the jury how to reach their verdict'.[19]

The key problem here is distinguishing between the last two, as they overlap.

John Dyson Heydon defined the 'legal burden' in these terms:

> The legal burden of proof is the obligation of a party to meet the requirement of a rule of law that a fact in issue be proved (or disproved) either by a preponderance of the evidence or beyond reasonable doubt ... The phrase 'legal burden' is that of Lord Denning and it is justified by the fact that its incidence is determined by the substantive law.[20]

In other words, there is a legal duty to prove certain things to make out the case. Failure to do so means that the legal element will fail, which carries the risk that the case will fail. For example, the prosecution must prove the specific elements of the offence and must disprove any defence(s) raised by the accused during the trial. The prosecution always carries this burden, except where the law imposes it on the accused. It is worth noting that it is unusual in the criminal law for the accused to have a legal burden of proof. This burden exists as a matter of law. Here, evidence is adduced during a trial for the purpose of establishing the elements of the offence. If this evidence is admissible and not contested, it operates to establish the legal burden at the conclusion of the case.

The 'evidential burden', by comparison, can be understood as:

> ... the obligation to show, if called on to do so, that there is sufficient evidence to raise an issue as to the existence or non-existence of a fact in issue.[21]

Broadly, this relates to the obligation to produce evidence in satisfaction of the elements of the offence or defence. In most cases the prosecution has the legal burden of proving the elements of the offence and disproving any defence(s), as well as an evidential burden in this respect. The defendant, on the other hand, generally only has an evidential burden with respect to raising a defence, at which point the prosecution has both an evidential and legal burden to disprove the existence of the defence.

The combination of these components was famously articulated in *Woolmington v DPP* by Viscount Sankey:

> Throughout the web of the English Criminal Law one golden thread is always to be seen, that *it is the duty of the prosecution to prove the prisoner's guilt subject*

18 Senate Standing Committee on Constitutional and Legal Affairs, *The Burden of Proof in Criminal Proceedings* (1982) in D Brown et al, *Criminal Laws* (The Federation Press, 7th ed, 2020) 249–51.

19 Ibid.

20 John Dyson Heydon, *Cross on Evidence* (Lexis Nexis, 9th ed, 2013) 265.

21 Ibid 266.

> *to* what I have already said as to *the defence of insanity* and subject also to *any statutory exception*. If, at the end of and on the whole of the case, there is a reasonable doubt, created by the evidence given by either the prosecution or the prisoner, as to whether the prisoner killed the deceased with a malicious intention, the prosecution has not made out the case and the prisoner is entitled to an acquittal. No matter what the charge or where the trial, the principle that the prosecution must prove the guilt of the prisoner is part of the common law of England and no attempt to whittle it down can be entertained.[22]

To a large extent, this distinction is almost pedantic. For present purposes, it is sufficient for you to be aware that there is an obligation for there to be evidence capable of establishing the elements of the law to the relevant threshold; that the duty of establishing the case (overall) rests with the prosecution; that the prosecution has an obligation to adduce evidence in order to establish each element during the course of the trial; and the accused may raise evidence that may establish defences. Further, defences may emerge out of the evidence itself, at which point the prosecution will be called on to adduce evidence tending to challenge that defence. And, for the sake of completion, the weight of evidence required in a prosecution case is beyond reasonable doubt, while the weight of evidence required by a defendant is on the balance of probabilities.

Figure 3.1 Burden of proof

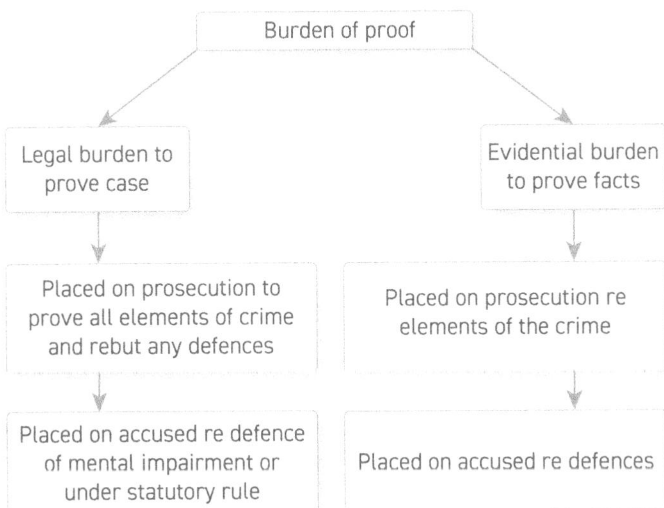

Source: Adapted from Simon Bronitt and Bernadette McSherry, *Principles of Criminal Law* (Thomson Reuters, 4th ed, 2017) 141.

22 *Woolmington v DPP* [1935] AC 462, 481–2 (emphasis added).

The standard of proof

The evidence presented in a court must be sufficiently coherent, relevant, and of a sufficient weight in order to satisfy the burden carried by the party at the relevant time. As outlined above, there are two 'standards of proof'. Proof relates to the presentation of evidence sufficiently convincing to confirm the existence of legally prescribed facts. The persuasive value of the evidence required varies according to whether or not a case is civil or criminal in nature.

The balance of probabilities is the 'civil standard' of proof. It is concerned with the concept that the evidence suggests that it is more likely than not that the asserted fact is in fact truthful. The civil standard arises in criminal cases where there is a burden of proof placed on the accused as a matter of law.

Beyond reasonable doubt is the 'criminal standard' of proof. It is concerned with the concept that the evidence establishes, to a high level of satisfaction, that the asserted fact is in fact truthful. In short, it is beyond doubt. This is not to say there may not be some degree of doubt, but if there is a reasonable or plausible doubt, then the threshold is not met. Where the accused has a legal burden, the obligation is satisfied at the lower 'civil' standard.

These standards have their origins in the common law and are now on a statutory footing in many jurisdictions. In New South Wales, for example, they are contained in the *Evidence Act 1995* (NSW).[23]

Balance of probabilities in civil proceedings

The statements above belie the complexity of each standard. Where the balance of probabilities is concerned, attention must be given to the nature of the matters being considered by the tribunal before it forms the view that the threshold has been met.

In *Neat Holdings v Karajan Holdings*, Mason CJ, Deane, Dawson and Gaudron JJ declared:

> The ordinary standard of proof required of a party who bears the onus in civil litigation in this country is proof on the balance of probabilities. That remains so even where the matter to be proved involves criminal conduct or fraud. On the other hand, the strength of the evidence necessary to establish a fact or facts on the balance of probabilities may vary according to the nature of what it is sought to prove. Thus, authoritative statements have often been made to the effect that clear or cogent or strict proof is necessary 'where so serious a matter as fraud is to be found'. Statements to that effect should not, however, be understood as directed to the standard of proof. Rather, they should be understood as merely reflecting a conventional perception that members of our society do not ordinarily engage in fraudulent or criminal conduct and a judicial approach that a court should not lightly make a finding that, on the balance of probabilities, a party to civil litigation has been guilty of such conduct.[24]

23 *Evidence Act 1995* (NSW) s 140 (civil standard of proof), s 141 (criminal standard of proof).
24 *Neat Holdings v Karajan Holdings* (1992) 110 ALR 449, 449–50 (footnotes omitted).

In *Qantas Airways v Gama*, Justice Branson stated:

> The correct approach to the standard of proof in a civil proceeding ... is that for which s 140 of the *Evidence Act* provides. It is an approach which recognises, adopting the language of the High Court in *Neat Holdings*, that the strength of the evidence necessary to establish a fact in issue on the balance of probabilities will vary according to the nature of what is sought to be proved – and, I would add, the circumstances in which it is sought to be proved.[25]

This principle on the weight of evidence necessary to satisfy the 'civil standard' is commonly known as the '*Briginshaw* standard', after the case of the same name. In *Briginshaw v Briginshaw*, Dixon J cautioned against assuming there was, in fact, more than one standard. He declared that the civil standard was 'fixed', but went on to say:

> Except upon criminal issues to be proved by the prosecution, it is enough that the affirmative of an allegation is made out to the reasonable satisfaction of the tribunal. But reasonable satisfaction is not a state of mind that is attained or established independently of the nature and consequence of the fact or facts to be proved. The seriousness of an allegation made, the inherent unlikelihood of an occurrence of a given description, or the gravity of the consequences flowing from a particular finding are considerations which must affect the answer to the question whether the issue has been proved to the reasonable satisfaction of the tribunal. In such matters 'reasonable satisfaction' should not be produced by inexact proofs, indefinite testimony, or indirect inferences.[26]

As we are concerned with the criminal law, the reference to s 140 does not ordinarily arise. It is included here because the terminology used is the same, and there is a good degree of overlap with the cases.

Balance of probabilities in criminal cases

You will note above that in criminal matters the standard of proof relating to the accused is expressed in s 141(2) of the *Evidence Act* but is also expressed as 'on the balance of probabilities'. This overlap has been recognised as problematic, because of the threshold expressed in *Briginshaw*, and the tendency of people to consider things in an actuarial manner when considering the differences between possibilities and probabilities. Bronitt and McSherry argue that the civil standard of proof in criminal cases has historically had little role to play, but with the proliferation of criminal sanctions in civil cases this standard is going to assume increasing importance, and will likely become the subject of future appeal.[27]

However, notwithstanding the limits of the test, the essence here is that there is sufficient evidence before the tribunal of fact to be satisfied there is at least *a reasonable possibility* of the fact asserted by the defendant.

25 *Qantas Airways v Gama* (2008) 167 FCR 537, [139].
26 *Briginshaw v Briginshaw* (1938) 60 CLR 336, 361.
27 See Simon Bronitt and Bernadette McSherry, *Principles of Criminal Law* (Thomson Reuters, 4th ed, 2017) 142–6.

A good discussion of the relationship between the respective burdens and their thresholds is outlined in *R v Youssef*:

> ... the Crown bears the onus of establishing each ingredient of the offence which has been charged. That is the 'golden thread' which runs throughout the web of the criminal law. That obligation of the Crown is subject to exception only in relation to the defence of mental illness (an exception to which I will return), and in cases where the onus of proof in relation to a particular issue is placed upon the accused by statute. In relation to every other issue which may arise at the trial, the Crown bears the onus of proof; many such issues are frequently (but misleadingly) called 'defences'.
>
> The Crown must therefore remove any reasonable possibility that the act of the accused was accidental, or that it was involuntary as a result of a state of automatism, or as a result of duress. The Crown must also remove any reasonable doubt raised by the accused's intoxication in determining whether the accused had formed the state of mind required for the offence charged; as well as any reasonable possibility that the act of the accused was provoked; or done in self-defence.
>
> That *legal* onus upon the Crown does not mean, however, that the Crown must bring evidence to meet every such 'defence' which could possibly arise in relation to the offence charged. In every case, the accused bears an *evidentiary* onus to point to or to produce evidence (or material in an unsworn statement) from which it could be inferred that — as I would prefer to put it — there is at least a reasonable possibility that, for example, the act of the accused was accidental, or that it was provoked or done in self-defence.
>
> The authorities make it clear that such a reasonable possibility must be shown by admissible evidence.[28]

Beyond reasonable doubt

As a matter of law, the courts have been reluctant to give any definition or guidance about the meaning of this term. It is a term that is left to the combination of information-based reasoning and intuition on the part of the tribunal of fact in the context of a criminal case. Various attempts to explain the idea to the jury over time have been attempted, but frequently those attempts have been overturned on appeal.[29]

Fundamentally, we are talking about a high threshold of proof sufficient to convince the decision maker. Again, academic commentary and scholars are critical of the idea, because there is a wide degree of tolerance for uncertainty among some, and none in

28 *R v Youssef* (1990) 50 A Crim R 1, 3 (footnotes omitted).

29 In Victoria some guidance is offered in pt 7 of the *Jury Directions Act 2015* (Vic). Where a jury requests it, the trial judge may give a direction on the scope of beyond reasonable doubt, although it remains limited. Section 61 of the *Jury Directions Act* provides: 'Unless an enactment otherwise provides, the only matters that the trial judge may direct the jury must be proved beyond reasonable doubt are – (a) the elements of the offence charged or an alternative offence; and (b) the absence of any relevant defence.'

others. Some people regard the threshold as requiring 'absolute proof', while others may think of the requirement as something just above 'more probable than not'.[30] Whatever the controversies, the courts tend to be quite conservative on the meanings, evidenced in cases such as *Green* and *Brooking*.

In *Green v R*, the High Court (Barwick CJ; McTiernan, Owen JJ) held:

> A reasonable doubt is a doubt which the particular jury entertain in the circumstances. Jurymen themselves set the standard of what is reasonable in the circumstances. It is that ability which is attributed to them which is one of the virtues of our mode of trial: to their task of deciding facts they bring to bear their experience and judgment. They are both unaccustomed and not required to submit their processes of mind to objective analysis of the kind proposed in the language of the judge in this case. 'It is not their task to analyse their own mental processes' ... A reasonable doubt which a jury may entertain is not to be confined to a 'rational doubt', or a 'doubt founded on reason' in the analytical sense ...[31]

Chief Justice Barwick later stated this more directly in *Keeley v Brooking* by simply stating:

> To be satisfied beyond all reasonable doubt is, for the purposes of the law, to be certain.[32]

USEFUL REFERENCE

Many courts publish bench books for ease of reference to the profession, which will include directions on these concepts.

In New South Wales the Judicial Commission has published a model direction, in the *Criminal Trial Courts Bench Book*, available through its website.

30 Bronitt and McSherry (n 27).
31 (1971) 126 CLR 28, 32.
32 (1979) 143 CLR 162, 169.

4 STATUTORY INTERPRETATION AND THE CRIMINAL LAW

A significant part of legal reasoning is linked to interpretation, and much of that process is shaped by the rules of interpretation. This is especially true in the criminal law, as most contemporary sources of law are located in legislation. The common law tradition has evolved an entire body of law specifically concerned with the interpretation of legislation, normally referred to as the 'law of statutory interpretation'. Those rules are found in a combination of common law case authorities and interpretation legislation. It is a significant area of law, and readers are referred to the major reference texts for further review.[1] This chapter introduces some of the core concepts underlying the statutory interpretation principles applicable to the criminal law.

General principles

By way of overview, in the context of working with criminal statutes, remember the following:

- The fundamental rules of statutory interpretation continue to apply.
- Broadly, that means the Act is read literally, but in the context of the whole, for the purpose of giving effect to the intention of Parliament.
- Focus on both *text* and *context.*
- 'Context' includes the textual context, as well as the policy applicable to the specific Act.

In a detailed analysis of the fundamental rules of interpretation of criminal statutes, Wood CJ at CL held in *R v Mailes*:

> [104] So far as any ambiguity arises ... I observe that, in accordance with authority, it is permissible to have regard to the long title so as to resolve any ambiguity ...
>
> [105] Similar principles apply to headings to Parts which can constrain the scope of a section contained within that Part where an ambiguity arises ...

1 Important reference texts on statutory interpretation include: Jeffrey Barnes, Jacinta Dharmananda and Eamonn Moran, *Modern Statutory Interpretation: Framework, Principles and Practice* (Cambridge University Press, 2023); M Sanson, *Statutory Interpretation* (Oxford University Press, 2nd ed, 2016); Kath Hall and Claire Macken, *Legislation and Statutory Interpretation* (Lexis Nexis, 5th ed, 2020); Lisa Burton Crawford et al, *Public Law and Statutory Interpretation: Principles and Practice* (The Federation Press, 2nd ed, 2021); Perry Herzfeld and Thomas Prince, *Statutory Interpretation Principles: The Laws of Australia* (Thomson Reuters, 2014).

> [106] Additionally, the purposive approach to statutory interpretation needs to be borne in mind when an ambiguity arises or where it is necessary to determine whether more than one interpretation is open ...
>
> [107] In this regard it is also trite law that it is open to have regard to the historical setting of the Statute in order to identify the object of the legislature ...
>
> [108] Finally, in relation to relevant principles of statutory interpretation, it is the case that where one or more Acts form a scheme of legislation, as in my view the *Health Act* and the *Procedure Act* do, it is proper to have regard to each of them for the purpose of construing expressions used in any one of them. Particularly is that appropriate where the Bills for the two Acts were introduced together and assented to on the same day, or where they have progressed in tandem ...[2]

An authoritative statement of principle is found in *Project Blue Sky v Australian Broadcasting Authority*:

> The primary object of statutory construction is to construe the relevant provision so that it is consistent with the language and purpose of all the provisions of the statute. The meaning of the provision must be determined 'by reference to the language of the instrument viewed as a whole'. In *Commissioner for Railways (NSW) v Agalianos*, Dixon CJ pointed out that 'the context, the general purpose and policy of a provision and its consistency and fairness are surer guides to its meaning than the logic with which it is constructed'. Thus, the process of construction must always begin by examining the context of the provision that is being construed.
>
> A legislative instrument must be construed on the prima facie basis that its provisions are intended to give effect to harmonious goals. Where conflict appears to arise from the language of particular provisions, the conflict must be alleviated, so far as possible, by adjusting the meaning of the competing provisions to achieve that result which will best give effect to the purpose and language of those provisions while maintaining the unity of all the statutory provisions.[3]

Generally, the terms in legislation can be categorised according to their meaning:

- ordinary meaning: terms that have a common meaning expressed in the English language
- defined meaning: terms that have a meaning expressed in the legislation, which may or may not have equivalent ordinary meaning
- contextual meaning: terms or concepts that are derived from looking at the provision in its statutory and policy context
- judicial meaning: terms that are derived from judicial decisions, normally in cases.

2 *R v Mailes* (2001) 53 NSWLR 251, 271 (per Spigelman CJ) (footnotes omitted).
3 (1998) 194 CLR 355, [69]–[70] (McHugh, Gummow, Kirby, Hayne JJ) (footnotes omitted).

These categories attract particular rules that will help in the process of interpretation. Knowing what those rules are, and accurate classification of the terms, is a crucial part of the process. One of the critical categories for the criminal law is recognising the fact that 'penal' provisions (that is, those that attract a state-enforced penalty up to and including imprisonment (or worse, in some jurisdictions)) have their own special rules of interpretation in addition to the core set of interpretation rules. As discussed in more detail below, the basic principle is that because of the consequences involved for an accused, penal provisions are normally treated more strictly than other forms of law. At its simplest, a penal statute is easily recognised where it has a specific penalty attached to it involving orders affecting the life, liberty or property of a person convicted for breach of the law.

Bennion defined penal statutes as any statute that 'inflicts hardship or deprivation of any kind on a person'.[4] The character of penal statutes in modern law is sometimes quite difficult to separate from civil law. As a general rule, any form of involuntary imposition of monetary penalty or deprivation of liberty could be characterised as a penal statute, even if it is ostensibly civil. It becomes more complex where the penalties are financial or administrative in character, and where the legislation is not clearly criminal. But for present purposes, the point is to give thought to the character of the matter, and whether the matter is properly categorised as penal, and work from there.

Interpretation Acts

It is important to remember the critical role that Interpretation Acts play in the interpretation of legislation. Historically the rules of statutory interpretation were sourced in the common law and equity, although over time there has been a tendency for these rules to be modified and placed in statute. Each jurisdiction in Australia has its own interpretation legislation.[5] This is true in most common law jurisdictions, including New Zealand,[6] Canada[7] and the United Kingdom.[8] In New South Wales, the relevant state law is the *Interpretation Act 1987* (NSW), with concurrent operation of the *Acts Interpretation Act 1901* (Cth) for federal matters. You should access and familiarise yourself with these Acts.

One of the key aspects of interpretation involves a consideration of extrinsic materials. This is of particular importance in the criminal law because it is often the only place where a clear sense of the intention of Parliament can be ascertained. In the criminal law one of the core matters of interest is the 'mischief' to which the Act or provision is directed. This is a very old rule of construction.[9] While much of the policy behind the criminal law is well settled, resort to the 'mischief rule' is not uncommon, especially where there are recent amendments and new pieces of legislation being

4 Francis Bennion, *Bennion on Statutory Interpretation* (Lexis Nexis, 5th ed, 2008) 784.
5 *Acts Interpretation Act 1901* (Cth); *Legislation Act 2001* (ACT); *Interpretation Act 1987* (NSW); *Interpretation Act 1978* (NT); *Acts Interpretation Act 1954* (Qld); *Acts Interpretation Act 1915* (SA); *Acts Interpretation Act 1931* (Tas); *Interpretation of Legislation Act 1984* (Vic); *Interpretation Act 1984* (WA).
6 *Legislation Act 2019* (NZ).
7 *Interpretation Act* (RSC 1985, c I-21).
8 *Interpretation Act 1889* (c 63); *Interpretation Act 1978* (c 30).
9 Known as the 'rule in Heydon's case'. See *Heydon's Case* (1584) 3 Co Rep 7a; 76 ER 637.

introduced. This can often be ascertained through reverting to the Second Reading Speeches of Parliament. In more recent years, it has become common for the objects of legislation to be embedded in the words of the statute, often in the first part of the Act. Where there is doubt, the golden rule for analysts is to check!

Special rules and principles that apply to criminal statutes

Because the criminal law is a mechanism that inflicts punishment and legitimises the exercise of state power, courts are required to pay close attention to the interpretation and application of statutes. This is particularly the case where the legislation presents a manifest error or ambiguity, or where it presents an apparent breach or abrogation of settled common law rights or immunities. In essence, the interpretation of criminal statutes requires the application of the core principles of statutory interpretation, as well as some specific rules that apply only to criminal statutes. Keep in mind that not every rule applies in every case.

Principle 1: Strict interpretation

The first principle is that criminal statutes are approached 'strictly', in the sense that where there is doubt or ambiguity, the default position is to adopt a position in favour of the accused.

> The law of England does not allow of offences by construction, and no case shall be holden to be reached by penal laws, but such as are within both the spirit and the letter of such laws' (*Blackstone's Commentaries*), a principle which remains part of the law ... notwithstanding the modification in the ancient strictness of its application which has occurred in the course of the modern search after the true nature of some actual legislative intention. No doubt, in determining whether an offence has been created or enlarged, the Court must be guided, as in other questions of interpretation, by the fair meaning of the language of the enactment, but when that language is capable of more than one meaning, or is vague or cloudy so that its denotation is uncertain and no sure conclusion can be reached by a consideration of the provisions and subject matter of the legislation, then it ought not to be construed as extending any penal category.[10]
>
> In determining the meaning of a penal statute the ordinary rules of construction must be applied, but if the language of the statute remains ambiguous or doubtful the ambiguity or doubt may be resolved in favour of the subject by refusing to extend the category of criminal offences. The rule is perhaps one of last resort.[11]
>
> [A]ny statute which authorises the detention of a person must be strictly construed.[12]

10 *R v Adams* (1935) 53 CLR 563, 567 (Rich, Dixon, Evatt and McTiernan JJ).
11 *Beckwith v The Queen* (1976) 135 CLR 569, 576 (Gibbs J).
12 *Williams v R* (1986) 161 CLR 278, 297.

The practical expression of the 'strict interpretation' rule has two limbs:

(1) 'In determining the meaning of a penal statute the ordinary rules of construction must be applied but, perhaps as a last resort, if the language of the statute remains ambiguous or doubtful the ambiguity or doubt may be resolved in favour of the subject by refusing to extend the category of criminal offences.'[13]
(2) 'In the event of ambiguity, a statute affecting the liberty of a person will be construed in favour of liberty.'[14]

It is important to remember that the duty of a court is to determine the case before it. Do not assume that just because there is an ambiguity in the interpretation of a statute that the court will just refuse to exercise jurisdiction. Courts have a constitutional duty to give effect to the will of Parliament expressed in the legislation. However, the idea of strict interpretation operates as both a rule and an orientation to interpretation. The orientation is that, so far as the law permits, an interpretation that favours the accused in cases of doubt should be adopted. The rule is that where legislation remains doubtful, or has an absurd outcome, then the court has discretion to dismiss the case.

This is not something that courts do lightly, and is, in fact, exceedingly rare. Even when it does happen, it is often the subject of an appeal. It is more common in the lower courts for matters to be referred to superior courts as a 'stated case', which is a process whereby the court will refer the matter to a superior court to answer specific questions of law.[15] Practically speaking it is rare for serious ambiguity to arise, especially where the law is 'settled'. Most cases going before courts are interpreted and applied without the need to engage in high-level interpretation. But even in cases where the law is 'settled', over time it is not unusual to find the need to interpret legislation in cases where recent amendments have been made that create anomalies and anachronisms in the structure of the law.[16] It is more usual for ambiguity to arise in cases where legislation is recent, or where the criminal law and civil law overlap, usually in the context of an ostensibly civil piece of legislation imposing sanctions.

Principle 2: Penalties are limited by legislation and the jurisdiction of the court

It is trite to say that courts may only impose penalties that are authorised by the law. It is a fundamental requirement of the rule of law that penalties may only be imposed by

13 Herzfeld and Prince (n 1) 260.

14 Ibid 263. See also *R v Adams* (1935) 53 CLR 563; *Beckwith v The Queen* (1976) 135 CLR 569; *Milne v The Queen* (2014) 88 ALJR 395.

15 Provisions exist in New South Wales for a case to be referred to the Supreme Court from the District Court pursuant to s 5B of the *Criminal Appeal Act 1912* (NSW).

16 For example, at common law murder required 'malice aforethought'. When the *Crimes Act 1900* (NSW) was introduced, it contained a definition of 'malice' (s 5), and a reference to malice in s 18(2)(a), a provision that enabled the distinction between murder and manslaughter. In 2008 the definition in s 5 was repealed, while the reference in s 18(2)(a) remained. The meaning of 'malice' was subsequently in doubt, later coming before the NSW Court of Criminal Appeal in 2016 (*R v IL* [2016] NSWCCA 51) and the High Court of Australia in 2017 (*IL v R* (2017) 345 ALR 375).

the state after due process of law if any punishment is to have domestic and international legitimacy.[17] The basic rule is that the penalties available to courts are variable. In Australia, the most serious form of penalty is incarceration. The *maximum* period of time that a person will serve is determined partly by maximum penalty set in legislation, and partly through the sentencing reasoning of judges. That reasoning involves an evaluation of the nature and extent of the offending.

In jurisdictions governed by a commitment to the rule of law there will be rules that clearly set out the imposition of penalties. In New South Wales, for example, s 18(1) of the *Crimes (Sentencing Procedure) Act 1999* (NSW) declares that where a penalty is specified in legislation, a court may impose a punishment *not exceeding* the penalty specified.

Courts are able to exercise a certain jurisdiction, depending on where they are in the hierarchy of the courts. Courts have jurisdictional limits on the types of matters they can deal with. Those limits not only restrict the kinds of matters a court can hear; they also impose caps on the penalties that can be applied. To understand this, it is useful to briefly review the hierarchy of the courts.

The common law world inherited a similar court structure through the reception of English law, which is typically modified and evolved according to local conditions, and following major reforms that took place in the 19th and 20th centuries. At its simplest, this is a tripartite division between Local or Magistrates' Courts, Crown Courts and Appellate Courts. This basic structure is the context in which most criminal law operates, with simple offences considered at the local level, trial cases at an intermediate level, and the most serious crimes, constitutional matters and complex appeals considered at the upper level of the hierarchy. Australia, as a federal system, also has a concurrent federal judicature. While there is a distinct body of Commonwealth criminal law, practically speaking most of those matters are determined in state courts.[18]

The essential court structure and associated jurisdictions for criminal matters in Australia are shown in Table 4.1.

The fundamental categories linked to the exercise of jurisdiction are the differences between an indictable offence, a summary offence, and an indictable offence triable summarily. An indictable offence must be heard in a trial court. Trial courts are heavily regimented with formal procedure, and normally involve presentation of the case to a jury, although it is becoming more common for trial matters to be considered by a judge sitting alone. Summary matters are heard in a Local or Magistrates' Court in the absence of a jury. Proceedings tend to be less formal and time consuming. The third category, indictable offences triable summarily, covers offences that can be determined by a trial court on the election of one of the parties. The default position is that such matters are decided summarily unless there is an election to proceed to trial. Jurisdiction is a fundamentally important aspect of analysis, as it determines what court the matter will be

17 Reflected in international instruments, such as arts 9 and 10 of the *Universal Declaration of Human Rights* (1948) and pt 3 of the *International Covenant on Civil and Political Rights* (1976).

18 It is worth noting there has been a growth in specialist courts over the last 25 years, including Drug Courts, Koori Courts and a restructuring of the Family Court.

Table 4.1 Simple hierarchy of the criminal courts in Australia

Court	Jurisdiction	Penalties
High Court of Australia	Unlimited. Can exercise original jurisdiction. Ultimate appellate court.	Unlimited, subject to statutory or common law limitation. Commonly remits sentencing matters to relevant state court.
State Supreme Court	Unlimited. Principal trial court for murder, treason and serious crimes. Functions as appeal court in state matters on questions of law.	Unlimited, subject to statutory or common law limitation. May remit matters to subordinate courts.
District/County Court	Principal trial court for indictable offences. Functions as appeal court in state matters for lower courts.	Unlimited, subject to statutory or common law limitation.
Local/Magistrates' Court	Principal court for matters triable summarily.	Jurisdiction limited by statute. Indictable matters disposed of summarily limited to maximum set by legislation (commonly two years' imprisonment).

determined in, which, in turn, shapes the nature of the proceedings and the kinds of penalties that may be ordered.[19]

The decision to make an election and proceed to trial has two practical effects. First, it engages a more formal trial process. Second, it immediately escalates the potential penalty that may be ordered by the court if convicted. Conversely, where the matter remains at the local level, proceedings are rather less formal, with an associated limitation on the maximum penalty available and a tendency to rely on written submissions as opposed to testimonial evidence.

The specific rules of procedure vary by jurisdiction, so it is worthwhile closely reviewing the relevant law. The key here is to be aware that the procedures in courts are heavily regulated by legislation, regulation, rules of court, common law and custom. The details of this are beyond the scope of this book. An overview is provided in the discussion on procedure in Chapter 5. The central rule is that a court has a discretion to impose a sentence proportionate to the gravity of the offending, capped by the jurisdictional limit of the court. The jurisdictional limit depends on what court is hearing the case. In general terms, a Local/Magistrates' Court has a jurisdictional limit of two years as a maximum penalty. This is so even where the maximum penalty under statute exceeds that cap. Matters that are indictable but dealt with summarily are subject to that jurisdictional limit, even if the offence might carry a higher maximum penalty in legislation. All other

19 Readers should familiarise themselves intimately with the courts and the procedures in which their matters will be considered. In New South Wales, for example, much of the law is sourced in the *Criminal Procedure Act 1986* (NSW).

courts are able to exercise jurisdiction to impose a penalty capped by the statutory common law maximum for an offence that that kind.

In addition to the general jurisdictional limits, it is important to remember there are limitation periods that can apply to causes of action in law. In the criminal law this is simple to state. As a rule, all indictable offences have an unlimited limitation period, lasting the full life of the perpetrator (and possibly after, if you believe in Divine Justice!). Summary offences, on the other hand, are normally time limited. In New South Wales, for example, such offences have a six-month limit from the date of the offence.[20]

Principle 3: Fundamental common law rights/liberties are not impugned except by express intention

Criminal law is packed with a range of procedural rules and principles that have evolved out of centuries of common law decisions that were designed to impose limitations on the cruelty of the law and the punishments that went with it.

One of the important rules in the interpretation of penal statutes is the presumption against removing common law rights:

> The insistence on express authorization of an abrogation or curtailment of a fundamental right, freedom or immunity must be understood as a requirement for some manifestation or indication that the legislature has not only directed its attention to the question of the abrogation or curtailment of such basic rights, freedoms or immunities but has also determined upon abrogation or curtailment of them. The courts should not impute to the legislature an intention to interfere with fundamental rights. Such an intention must be clearly manifested by unmistakable and unambiguous language. General words will rarely be sufficient for that purpose if they do not specifically deal with the question because, in the context in which they appear, they will often be ambiguous on the aspect of interference with fundamental rights.[21]

But remember that Parliament has power to abrogate those rights, subject to the *Australian Constitution*. Complexities can arise in these cases where there is doubt as to the existence and/or nature of the right. In New South Wales, for example, there is no explicit statement of public rights. That is no accident, as the existence and nature of rights is widely regarded as being found in the common law and largely political in nature. This is not to suggest that there are no 'rights' in New South Wales. For practical purposes most of the rights enjoyed by the public are embedded in procedural statutes.[22] This is to be contrasted with other jurisdictions, such as Victoria, that have an explicit human rights statute.[23] Australians expect a set of procedural and substantive rights

20 *Criminal Procedure Act 1986* (NSW) s 179.
21 *Coco v The Queen* (1994) 179 CLR 427, 437 (Mason CJ, Brennan, Gaudron, McHugh JJ).
22 See, eg, the *Law Enforcement (Powers and Responsibilities) Act 2002* (NSW), especially pt 9.
23 *Charter of Human Rights and Responsibilities Act 2006* (Vic).

common to liberal democracies, articulated in international instruments and theory.[24] Those principles include:

- equality before the law
- freedom from arbitrary arrest
- freedom from forced work
- freedom of association
- freedom of movement
- freedom of speech and expression
- freedom of thought, conscience, religion and belief
- humane treatment by authorities
- protection from retrospective criminal law
- protection from torture and cruel, inhumane or degrading treatment
- protection of cultural and property rights
- recognition and protection of family life and children
- right not to be punished more than once
- right to a fair trial
- right to liberty and security of the person
- right to life
- right to peaceful assembly, demonstration and petition
- right to privacy and reputation
- right to take part in public life
- special protections of the vulnerable in the criminal process.

IMPORTANT REFERENCES

United Nations Declaration of Human Rights
International Covenant on Civil and Political Rights

Principle 4: Presumption against retrospectivity

Because much of the criminal law depends on legislation, it is presumed that legislation does not make things criminal prior to the commencement date of that Act. The fundamental rule is that legislation is intended to regulate the future rather than the past. Because criminal laws impose penalties, it is manifestly unfair to subject a person to punishments for things they did in the past that were legal at the time they were committed. However, this is a rebuttable presumption:

> The resistance of the law to retrospectivity in legislation is to be found in the rule that, save where the legislature makes its intention clear, a statute ought

24 For a scholarly examination on rights in the criminal justice system in Australia see Jeremy Gans et al, *Criminal Process and Human Rights* (Federation Press, 2011).

> not be given a retrospective operation where to do so would be to attach new legal consequences to facts or events which occurred before its commencement ... However, the injustice which might be inflicted by construing an enactment so as to give it a retrospective operation may vary according to its subject matter. Indeed, justice may lay almost wholly upon the side of giving remedial legislation a retrospective operation where that is possible ... With legislation of that character, if the ordinary rule be couched in terms of a presumption against retrospectivity, it must, at best, be a weak presumption ... With a criminal law, where the injustice of giving it an ex post facto operation will ordinarily be readily apparent, the presumption must be at its strongest.[25]

The key here is that Parliament does have the power and authority to create laws with retrospective effect and application. However, because that action triggers the presumption against retrospectivity, such laws will be read strictly against that construction unless there is explicit intention expressed by Parliament.

Principle 5: The presumption of mens rea

You will be aware that many pieces of legislation contain no reference to a 'fault element'. This is a common feature of criminal statutes, and presents something of an enduring problem in the criminal law: what state of mind must be proven, if at all, to convict the accused?

The general rule is that mens rea is presumed to be present, even where it is not mentioned in the legislation. That is a rebuttable presumption, determined through a process of statutory interpretation. It is a concept of some complexity because it involves a number of potential outcomes.

Herzfeld and Prince summarised the principle: 'Mens rea is an essential element in every statutory office unless, having regard to the language of the statute and to its subject matter, it is excluded expressly or by necessary implication.'[26]

This statement, while accurate, does not adequately explain the underlying complexities. The leading Australian authority on point is *He Kaw Teh v The Queen.*[27] This case was an appeal against conviction for importing 2.7 kilograms of heroin pursuant to s 233B(1) of the *Customs Act 1901* (Cth). Two charges were involved: one of importing a prohibited import, and the other of being in possession of a prohibited import. The problem that existed was that the provision made no reference to any requirement to prove a fault element. The offence was apparently complete on the physical elements of the offence, namely the act of importation and possession of a prohibited import.[28]

25 *Polyukhovich v The Commonwealth* (1991) 172 CLR 501, 650 (Dawson J).

26 Herzfeld and Prince (n 1) 265.

27 *He Kaw Teh v The Queen* (1985) 157 CLR 523.

28 At the time s 233B(1)(b) and (c) read: 'Any person who – (b) imports, or attempts to import, into Australia any prohibited imports to which this section applies or exports, or attempts to export, from Australia any prohibited exports to which this section applies; or (c) without reasonable excuse (proof whereof shall lie upon him) has in his possession, or attempts to obtain possession of, any prohibited imports to which this section applies which have been imported into Australia in contravention of this Act; ... shall be guilty of an offence.'

In what is a rather densely written decision, the common law presumption of mens rea was confirmed by the High Court, with Gibbs CJ articulating aspects of the operation of the presumption:

> The rule is not always easy to apply. Its application presents two difficulties – first, in deciding whether the Parliament intended that the forbidden conduct should be punishable even in the absence of some blameworthy state of mind and secondly, if it is held that mens rea is an element of the offence, in deciding exactly what mental state is imported by that vague expression.[29]
>
> In deciding whether the presumption has been displaced ... and whether the Parliament intended that the offence created by that provision should have no mental ingredient, there are a number of matters to be considered.
>
> First ... one must have regard to the words of the statute creating the offence.
>
> The second matter to be considered is the subject matter with which the statute deals.
>
> A third consideration is ... whether putting the defendant under strict liability will assist in the enforcement of the regulations. That means there must be something he can do, directly or indirectly ... which will promote the observance of the regulations.
>
> These cases establish that if it is held that guilty knowledge is not an ingredient of an offence, it does not follow that the offence is an absolute one. A middle course, between imposing absolute liability and requiring proof of guilty knowledge or intention, is to hold that an accused will not be guilty if he acted under an honest and reasonable mistake as to the existence of facts, which, if true, would have made his act innocent.[30]

In a separate decision, Brennan J similarly considered the problems of ascertaining whether the presumption was rebutted, and in particular of ascertaining the nature of mens rea:

> However grave the mischief at which a statute is aimed may be, the presumption is that the statute does not impose criminal liability without mens rea unless the purpose of the statute is not merely to deter a person from engaging in prohibited conduct but to compel him to take preventive measures to avoid the possibility that, without deliberate conduct on his part, the external elements of the offence might occur. A statute is not so construed unless effective precautions can be taken to avoid the possibility of the occurrence of the external elements of the offence.
>
> It is one thing to say that *mens rea* is an element of an offence: it is another to say precisely what is the state of mind required.[31]

Fundamentally, the decision in *He Kaw Teh* creates three categories of offences: (1) offences in which there is an explicit requirement to prove a fault element (mens rea),

29 *He Kaw Teh v The Queen* (1985) 157 CLR 523, 528.
30 Ibid 528–9.
31 Ibid 564–5.

(2) offences where mens rea on the part of the accused is presumed unless they can show an honest and reasonable belief the conduct was not criminal and (3) offences that require no proof of mens rea.[32] As explained by Brown et al:

> It is now generally accepted that category 2 offences can ... be described as imposing *strict* liability, while category 3 offences are labelled offences of *absolute* liability. ... Following the decision in *He Kaw Teh*, the focus in the case law has been on whether statutory offences which are silent on the question of mens rea should be classified as falling into category 2 or 3, and the usual approach is to put them in category 2.[33]

The process of characterisation of mens rea is not easy, and is one of the more difficult tasks to be learned, as Figure 4.1 illustrates.

32 *Wampfler v R* (1987) 11 NSWLR 541, 546 (Street CJ).

33 David Brown et al, *Criminal Laws: Materials and Commentary on Criminal Law and Process of New South Wales* (Federation Press, 7th ed, 2020) 207.

Figure 4.1 The rebuttable presumption of mens rea at common law

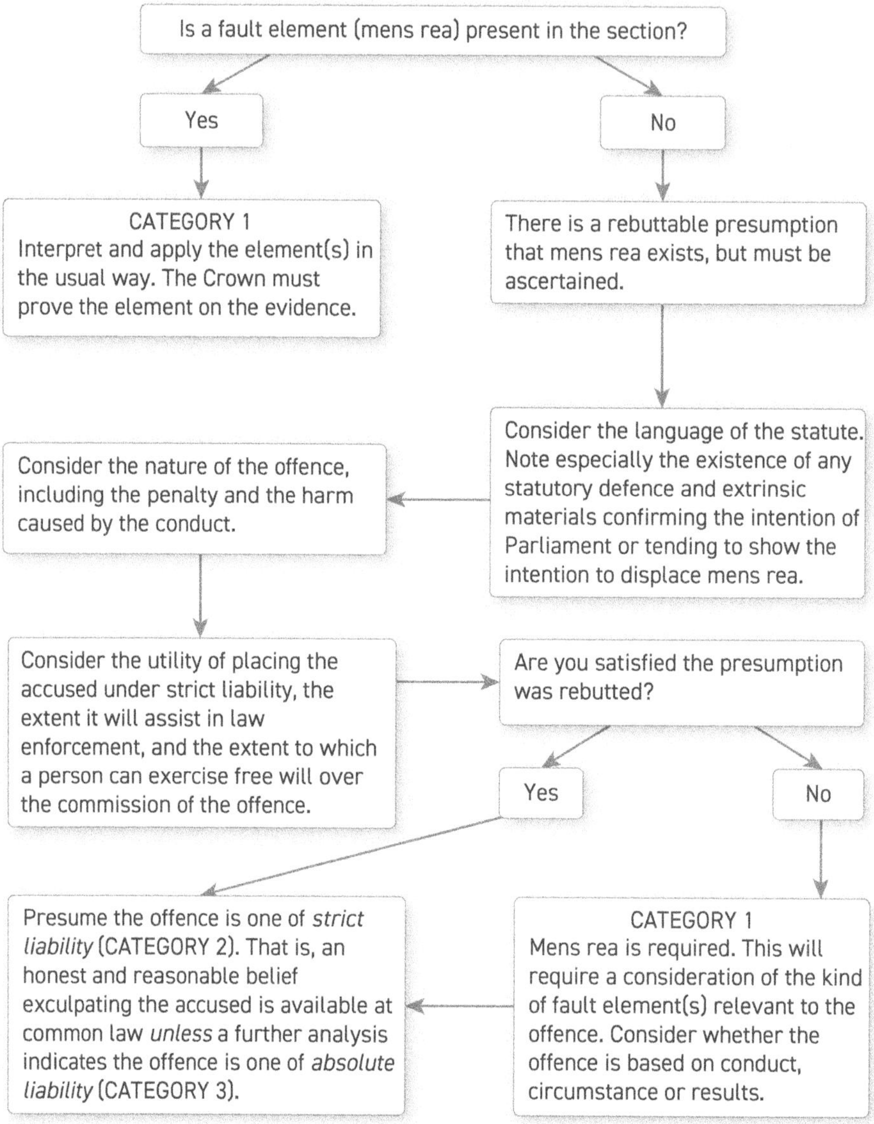

ANALYSING A PROBLEM

5

Problem solving is an art form, which takes years of practice, experience, a thorough understanding of the law and a sound understanding of human behaviour. This chapter presents some basic ideas to set you on the path.

Legal problem solving begins with being presented with information requiring an explanation of a suitable course of action, based on predictive reasoning. The task is often simply one of being asked 'faced with this scenario, what is the legal outcome?'. There are several steps involved in dealing with a problem. Please keep in mind that legal reasoning is not linear, although it can be. Much depends on the nature of the problem. It involves the ability to follow a linear, logical approach in some cases, and a tentative, nomadic approach in others. At its core is the ability to reason in uncertainty

In this chapter we explore strategies for problem solving. Up to now we have talked about a way of thinking about law and fact in the context of analysing problems. At this point we move the discussion towards application. Two approaches are suggested: one basic, the other advanced.

Both approaches are outlined here. The model you choose really depends on your *purpose* and the depth of analytical *detail* needed. The basic model is a useful starting point to begin learning the skill and provides a quicker path to problem solving - very useful in exams when you have limited time, and equally useful when looking at a brief for the first time. However, it is a model that provides a relatively shallow examination most of the time and is best suited as a preliminary mode of thinking as opposed to the deep-level analysis we have been discussing.

Basic problem analysis

Basic problem analysis is normally undertaken via an approach that involves four or five steps and is often presented in acronym form to assist in memory retention. As discussed in Chapter 1, there are dozens of models, the most common of which are 'ILAC' and 'MIRAT'. 'ILAC' stands for 'Issues', 'Law', 'Argument' and 'Conclusion';[1] while 'MIRAT' stands for 'Material Facts', 'Issues', 'Rules', 'Application' and 'Tentative Conclusion'.[2] These acronyms reflect a methodology that is broadly similar to judicial reasoning.

1 Michael Brogan and David Spencer, *Becoming a Lawyer: Success at Law School* (Oxford University Press, 3rd ed, 2014).
2 John Wade, 'Meet MIRAT: Legal Reasoning Fragmented into Learnable Chunks' (1991) 2(1) *Legal Education Review* 283; Patrick Keyzer, *Legal Problem Solving: A Guide for Law Students* (LexisNexis Butterworths, 2nd ed, 2003).

While providing a useful model for organising the intellectual content, these models are actually representations of a very complex form of reasoning. As discussed in Chapter 1, these models have weaknesses. Notwithstanding that, knowing a basic model for problem analysis is critical to start learning the process. It enables a rapid appraisal of your subject and is particularly useful as a tool when under time pressure (such as an exam). As these models are well known and readily available, they will not be discussed further. Students wanting to master the art are advised to read broadly and refer to the recommended readings at the end of the chapter. While these techniques are useful guides for learning, the problem with them is that they are very much introductory models that tend to produce limited, simple answers. Indeed, as you progress through law school there is an expectation that your analytical skills will grow and develop. Senior students and entry-level practitioners are expected to move beyond simply dividing information into simple headings aligned with the acronym. These are not a checklist. They are mnemonics intended to jog the memory and organise complexity.

It is useful to unpack some of the important elements of these models to develop a more nuanced approach.

Issues

What are 'issues'? Brogan and Spencer suggest that '[t]he issue in a case is the question of law to be decided by the court'.[3] John Wade argues that the 'I' in 'MIRAT' refers to 'issues in law and policy' but doesn't give concrete examples. He suggests that 'issues are often stated as rhetorical questions', which can exist at a micro or macro level, unfolding gradually as the analysis progresses.[4] The difficulty with both these authors' statements is that the issues are not always linked to a question of law, and neither is the focus always linked to a rhetorical question. Issues may exist within the law, within the facts, and in the interaction of both. These tend to be interwoven in the analysis.

For example, in the criminal law context, the ultimate issue is whether an accused person is guilty of a charged crime. That is a question of fact decided by the tribunal of fact. Issues of law and policy may form part of the analysis. A rhetorical question may be 'Is X guilty of murder?'. An open-ended question may be 'Discuss the criminal liability of X', which is not a rhetorical question. What is needed is a degree of adaptability and an ability to identify and think through the fact and law matrix and its unique combination. A discussion on criminal liability may integrate rhetorical questions, as shown in Figure 5.1.

Legal analysis depends primarily on an empirical foundation. That empirical foundation is made up of the available evidence representing the facts, and the law relevant to the cause of action. There is a relationship between the two. The facts trigger a range of legalities. The legalities will then direct precisely what is to be done with the facts.

3 Michael Brogan and David Spencer, *Surviving Law School* (Oxford University Press, 2nd ed, 2008) 92.
4 Wade (n 2) 286–7.

Figure 5.1 Unpacking a discussion question on criminal liability

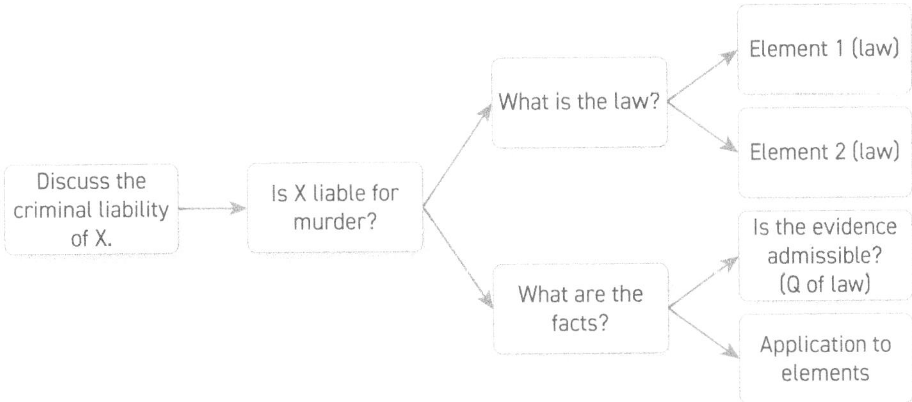

The problem in law is that the 'fact' may be contested, denied, qualified or not captured by some form of record that enables it to be presented to a court. Where the evidence is denied or not available, that is an 'issue' in the facts. Issues in the facts need to be resolved. Resolution then depends on thinking through what is missing, determining interpretations open on the available facts and advising on what needs to be done, if anything, to inform the court. That analysis is qualified by the law relevant to the problem. The law relevant to the problem imports its own possible problems. *The issues may therefore be understood as the legal and factual uncertainties present in the task.*

For example, let's say that your client has been charged with causing the death of a person while driving under the influence of alcohol. A blood sample taken soon after the accident may have been taken in breach of the law regulating the timing of the sample. The blood sample is direct evidence of intoxication, but the breach of law in taking the sample may result in that evidence being inadmissible. This is an important issue that needs to be considered, with the possible outcomes explained.

Material facts

What are the 'material facts'? This is actually a deceptive concept. Wade argues that 'A material fact can be described as a fact of vital importance to a line of deductive reasoning in order to solve a problem or to give helpful advice on a range of options'.[5] The most common trap for novice analysts is to undertake a 'surface reading' of the information in front of them. The key word in Wade's model is 'vital'. A fact has 'vital' importance where it is directly linked to a *legal* proposition. In many cases the *law* is invisible without undertaking research, and what initially appeared to be important or definitive may, in fact, be unimportant or even legally invalid. *What is a material fact will depend on the law that governs it.* That means that the analyst is always engaged in a flexible process of moving between the facts and the law in a constant process of evaluation.

5 Ibid 285.

Rules

The expression 'rules' is problematic. Lawyers are interested in *relevant law*, not simply 'rules'. The difference between them cannot be overstated. Law has coercive force through the mobilisation of institutional power. *What is 'relevant'*, as we have seen, *is information in fact and law that establishes a process or outcome with coercive consequence.* A 'rule', on the other hand, is a general term that captures law, but extends into principles, norms and guidelines, most of which do not have coercive institutional power as their operative core. It would therefore be far more useful to think about 'rules' as *relevant law*. In that context it is equally important to have a broad understanding of the nature of law. The law in some cases may be sourced in legislation and/or case authority, but can also be sourced in delegated legislation, such as regulations, and sometimes codes of conduct. But in each case what distinguishes a formal and an informal rule is the fact that formal rules will have a source rooted in a specific law or statutory instrument as opposed to mere custom or norm.[6]

Advanced problem analysis

A more nuanced approach to analysis requires something beyond mechanical logic. It requires a different way of thinking. To understand this approach, it is helpful to think about the nature of knowledge and the process of reasoning, sourced in Aristotelian philosophy. Aristotle conceived of three intellectual virtues, or forms of knowledge. The first he referred to as 'episteme'. This is a stable and context-independent form of knowledge, such as a mathematic equation or scientific observation. It is based on observation, replication and common experience. The second he called 'techne', a form of knowledge based on practical application and production of objects. It is context-dependent and passed on through demonstration and experience. The third form of knowledge he called 'phronesis'. Phronetic knowledge is context-dependent and directed towards prediction and action. It operates at the individual level (such as household management), but also the state level. Importantly, applied phronesis at the state level is linked to public policy and 'legislative science' ('nomothetike'). It is a concept that is concerned with political stability through ethical and prudent decision making in a particular context. Whereas epistemic knowledge is stable and has universal application, phronetic knowledge is applied on a case-by-case basis, potentially achieving variable outcomes, the merits of which are value-laden and ethically practical.[7] These three forms of knowledge are useful starting points for understanding the nature of judicial and legal reasoning, as the problem-solving technique is mainly a form of phronesis.

The phronetic approach involves a degree of 'dextrous' or 'nomadic' thought that is not bound by rigid thinking. It requires an adaptive approach that promotes conceptual movement between the simple and the complex and being conscious of the difference. But not only is this kind of thinking about adaptation and conceptual dexterity; it is also

6 Custom and norms have a complex relationship with law and policy and have particular effect in the context of private and public international law. For present purposes we will note that and move on.

7 Aristotle, *Nicomachean Ethics*, tr H Rackman (Harvard University Press, 1934) 344–7; Bent Flyvbjerg, *Making Social Science Matter: Why Social Inquiry Fails and How It Can Succeed Again* (Cambridge University Press, 2001) 55–60.

a form of reasoning with an ethical core – a sense of the *justice* of the outcome.[8] At this point it is worth noting that there is a difference between a legally correct outcome and a 'just' outcome, as justice and law are sometimes at odds. Ideally, justice and law are aligned but frequently human beings confuse justice with getting what they want.

A more nuanced approach to thinking about a legal problem involves a detailed consideration of discrete components within the facts and associated law. Those components may be identified as follows:

- Are you working from the law to the facts, or from the facts to the law?
- What jurisdiction is involved?
- What are the harms?
- What are the procedures?
- What is the scope of law involved?
- What are the elements of the cause of action?
- What does an initial interpretation suggest?
- What evidence is available or missing?
- What is the nature and strength of the evidence?
- Are there weak or stronger conclusions?
- Are there factual uncertainties that need to be resolved?
- Are there legal uncertainties that need to be resolved?
- Are there any defences or counterclaims available?
- Are there alternative outcomes?
- Are there specific procedural considerations?
- What are the outcomes (such as sentencing)?

This list suggests there is a particular sequence to be followed. That is not the case. The essence of a phronetic approach to reasoning is to be flexible and willing to move back and forth through the process. Sometimes your analysis will evolve at a late stage, which may mean you need to revisit early phases in the analysis. This is especially true in hard cases where there are multiple complexities. But if the matter is a narrow one, your reasoning may well follow a less complex and linear approach. We will now consider each step in more detail.

Apply law to facts, or facts to law?

As discussed above, there are two ways of beginning the preliminary analysis. Either you know what the law in play is at the outset, or you don't. The complexity in law is such that even when you think you know, you are assuming that to be correct. Often it is, but sometimes it's not. (For example, you may have been served with a court attendance notice alleging breaches of the *Crimes Act* – but unless you are aware to the fact the relevant section is unconstitutional, then you are missing something of vital importance.)

8 Flyvbjerg (n 7); Bent Flyvbjerg, Todd Landman and Sanford Schram (eds), *Real Social Science: Applied Phronesis* (Cambridge University Press, 2012); Brendon Murphy and Jeff McGee, 'Phronetic Legal Inquiry: An Effective Design for Law and Society Research?' (2015) 24(2) *Griffith Law Review* 288.

In the first instance, you begin by identifying the specific laws that are relied on and proceed by interpreting these. In the context of the criminal law, you may, for example, have been provided with notice of a person being charged with one or more specific offences. Here your analysis necessarily begins with the section(s) identified. You would, however, be alert to other possibilities.

In the second instance you have to begin with the facts that are available to you, and scope what the likely law is that may apply to those facts. This second stage is more difficult, because it demands a sound knowledge of the law. Here the facts will point towards a range of possibilities logically connected with the nature of the facts.

Jurisdiction

The *first* question that needs to be asked is concerned with *jurisdiction*. Jurisdiction is concerned with who has lawful authority to decide the case. That is, what law applies, and what court has authority to hear the matter if this case proceeded to court? In the criminal law there is a deceptively simple rule linked to the *geographic nexus*. Basically, the law of a state will apply to the accused where some criminal act was committed wholly or partly in that state, or some conduct of the accused outside the state had an effect within the state. Most of the time there is no issue – the accused committed a crime in a location wholly within the geographic territory of a state.[9] But sometimes things get complicated, namely where things happen across boundaries or where federal law applies. A legal complexity arises whenever there is some action that involves crossing a legal border. For example, a person might commit an offence in Victoria and be arrested in New South Wales. The border issue now involves a question about what the person can be charged with, or related procedural questions linked to extradition, depending on the facts. If federal law is involved, there might be concurrent state and Commonwealth matters to consider, as is sometimes the case with drug offences or family law matters.

In addition to thinking about what law applies, it is important to consider what court has authority to deal with the case. It's very common for inexperienced legal analysts to overlook *where* the case would be decided. As discussed earlier, there is a division of courts that can decide certain matters. Both issues are threshold questions when scoping the relevant law. Finally, give some thought to the parties in the case. Most of the time there will be no issue here. Most parties are adults and often legally represented. However, you might find that because of the *age* of the accused the matter is dealt with in a specialist children's court (in a criminal case) or require special rules for a nominated representative to conduct proceedings on their behalf. In these ways the facts of the case and the applicable law will help identify important questions of jurisdiction.

Identify the harms and procedures

A useful starting point with 'fact' analysis is to focus on the 'harms' that are evident in the facts, whether they be past, present, or future, and whether they be personal or proprietary. Injuries, damage, destruction, violence, obscenity, and sinister agreements are all

9 See, eg, *Crimes Act 1900* (NSW) pt 1A.

indicia of potential forms of criminality, and useful guides to point you in the direction of rules with consequence. It is important to note that here we are speaking about *substantive* law – that is, that body of criminal law concerned with prohibitions. This is to be contrasted with *procedural* law. When thinking through procedural law you will be looking for facts that indicate that required procedures have not been followed, or identifying conduct that needs to be followed. The distinction is one of past, present or future activity. Identifying the harms is an excellent first step in scoping the law if you don't know what charge is likely to arise, while knowing what the person has been charged with will inform your appraisal of the harms. In the context of civil matters, it may be that your task is mobilising the court for a specific purpose. Let's say your task involves considering an injunction. Here the rules linked to the specific injunction will require certain kinds of pleadings, forms and evidence necessary to support the cause of action.

Practice tip: Chronologies

An extremely useful tool for reasoning over time is the chronology. Setting out a timeline that identifies what happened, when, where and involving whom is often an effective way of developing a theory around the case. It can be critical in determining and resolving a number of legal issues that can arise in relation to proximity, temporal links and sometimes causation.

Scope the law

Scoping the law really depends on your knowledge of the law itself. At a minimum, you will need to know the core statutes that govern the field in your jurisdiction. Practically speaking, in Australia the core of the criminal law is located in a limited number of statutes, with a Commonwealth overlay (although it has limited application). Here you are asking yourself, 'What law potentially applies to the problem?' As we have considered this as a threshold question, it is useful to return to that at this stage once you have considered the harms. That will usually have the effect of confirming the jurisdiction questions.

Now, this step relates only to *liability* questions. The thing to remember is there is a vast amount of *procedural* law that can apply. For present purposes we will not discuss this aspect, but keep in mind that procedural law will also play a key role – especially those rules that have consequences linked to court process, bail and sentencing. We consider that under 'Procedural considerations' and 'Sentencing' below.

Identify the elements of the proposed offence

Once you have identified plausible offences, the next step involves approaching each possibility, one at a time, with a specific view to identifying the elements of the offence or cause of action. As discussed, the elements of the offence are those components sourced in the law that must be supported by the admissible evidence to establish as facts beyond reasonable doubt by the prosecution (in most cases). This needs to be a *methodical* and *systematic* process. As discussed in Chapter 2, identifying the elements of an offence, or cause of action, involves a careful reading of the source of law, with specific regard to the operative parts of the source. In the criminal law it means being alert to identifying the physical components of a statement, such as conduct, circumstances and results, combined with expressions linked to the state of mind of the person, usually expressed as intention, knowledge, recklessness or negligence. If in doubt, refer back to Chapter 2. Other forms of law will not have statements with criminal consequence. They may, for example, be procedural in nature, or declaratory of meaning or authority. Regardless of the nature of the provision being considered, the art of legal reasoning involves a close reading of text alive to the operative part and meaning of statements.

Preliminary interpretation

The next step involves clarifying in your mind what the elements are, as a matter of law, by interpreting the section, with particular attention to unpacking the law within each element. You do not need to go into detail at this stage – merely have enough actual knowledge of the law to be able to identify the appropriate evidence in the facts that may or may not satisfy these elements, and know what the relevant factual or legal issues are in the problem. Novices will need to spend a lot more time doing this than experts. The aim is to inform yourself during the consideration stage to be able to confidently explain what is going on with each element. Only by undertaking an *exhaustive* study early in your learning will you develop the required working knowledge to become efficient. Over time and through practice, the level of knowledge expands with application and experience, until (ideally) the level of knowledge and competence becomes fully integrated and true expertise begins to develop and emerge. The person with expertise will be equipped to undertake a preliminary assessment very quickly, rapidly identifying the stable and predictable law and facts within the situation, and able to recognise the gaps and hidden areas that are not obvious to the novice.

Identify the evidence

Once you are clear about the elements of the offence or cause of action and the general nature of the law for each element, you are in a position to identify the particular components of evidence necessary for your analysis. The harm evaluation already undertaken will point you towards the law initially, but here you are returning to the evidence to make an evaluation of the aspects of the matrix that are actually relevant to the task.

Associate and evaluate the elements and the evidence

Here, you go through a process of associating each relevant piece of evidence with the appropriate elements in law, and then begin to evaluate the outcome of that association. You are considering an array of things, such as whether you have clear, unequivocal or uncontested evidence that matches the requirements of the elements in law; what evidence is missing; and what evidence is contested or doubtful. Similarly, you will also consider the extent to which the evidence does not satisfy the requirements in law, and if so, what that means for your case.

Reject the weak, embrace the strong

As part of your evaluation, you will want to rule out those charges that you *know* do not apply, as well as those that are *plausible* and those that are *certain*. Remember, you must always keep the standard and burden of proof in mind. Doing so will assist in making this evaluation. One of the common errors that novice analysts make is trying to deal with *everything* that might be in a briefing. In the context of a word-limited assessment task, that approach can be a disaster because it routinely means that the discussion is so thin that it lacks meaningful engagement with the law. That becomes an issue for students, because it is very often the case that most of the marks assigned to the assessment are directly linked to meaningful discussion of the relevant law – so the 'shotgun' approach might hit your target, but the rest of it is irrelevant and superficial. If losing marks is the only thing you care about, then that is reason enough to avoid doing it. From a practitioner's perspective, the result is even worse because you can end up prosecuting or defending the wrong charge, wasting the time of the court, and exposing yourself and your client to unnecessary costs. In the worst-case scenario there are professional conduct implications for you linked to competent practice. Remember the threshold consideration is *relevance*.

Resolve factual uncertainties

Part of your reasoning needs to consider the nature of the evidence, inconsistencies, gaps and controversies. This process involves not only identifying these as potential issues, but also what the uncertainty means, and what can be done about it (if anything). This aspect of reasoning in uncertainty is one of the essential characteristics of legal thinking. It is a process of ascertaining and making clear the unknown, as well as persuading a court about the correct resolution of uncertainty through the power of submissions and argument.

Resolve legal uncertainties

As you proceed with the analysis, you will be reading and referring to the relevant law that applies in the case. In that process you may identify instances where the law itself is an issue because of a range of matters, such as ambiguous interpretation, conflicting authorities and sometimes related questions linked to the operation of other areas of law. For example, the law in the case might have constitutional implications, or enliven human rights provisions found in other statutes. So, in addition to the resolution of factual uncertainty, part of your reasoning will need to attend to the problems that are either inherent in the law itself or arise from some issue in the application of the facts to the law in the present case. In most cases that resolution will involve a more detailed analysis of the law than you had initially undertaken. Keep in mind that in some cases the resolution of the problem may be a matter for subsequent judicial clarification (eg an appeal or stated case) or depend on the exercise of judicial discretion (eg the admissibility of evidence). In these cases you may have no clear answer at hand, other than the identification of a matter of significant legal uncertainty that will require related judicial clarification. Here the task becomes one of thinking through the possible outcomes of one resolution or another. What happens if the courts decide one outcome, as opposed to another?

Defence(s)

No consideration of a legal problem is complete without attending to the potential availability of a defence or counterclaim available to the accused or respondent. In some cases, there may be clear liability for the charge you have identified, but a defence may have the capacity of excusing the accused partially or totally, and is of fundamental importance in any analysis. Very often such matters will not be stated or obvious, and again rely heavily on a broad understanding of the area of law. Even when you are aware of the specific allegation in a criminal or civil case, remember that it is not the prosecutor's job to answer their own allegation – that is the task of the respondent. When thinking about a problem it is just as important in the discussion to think about how a cause of action/charge could be answered on the available law and facts.

Alternatives

You will want to consider the alternative(s) that may apply in the present case. In some instances, the alternative is embedded in the law by way of a statutory alternative verdict, but in other cases you will need to repeat the process to identify the other possibilities where they exist from an opposing point of view. This kind of 'reversal in thinking' is a powerful analytical tool because it forces you to question and attack your own proposition and reasoning — a process that can highlight weaknesses in evidence, faulty or alternative interpretations of law, and cast doubt on an assumed resolution.

Procedural considerations

As mentioned earlier, procedural considerations are important. There are three dimensions at play with *procedure*. The first is linked to the *charge in court*. The second is linked to *pre-trial police processes* and the third relates to *evidence*. The extent to which you embark on this kind of analysis will vary. The *charge in court* is an essential consideration because you must be aware of whether the offence is strictly indictable, a summary offence or an indictable offence triable summarily. *Pre-trial police processes* may or may not be an issue. Things such as the nature of any arrest, the use of warrants, the conduct of police and the legality of any interview are important considerations because they may enliven intervention options linked to the admissibility of evidence, the strength of the evidence, and tort action against police. This overlaps with questions on *evidence*. If the evidence is inadmissible, then there may be no case to answer. These aspects of problem solving are advanced concepts and depend on a level of knowledge beyond most introductory courses, but from a practitioner perspective are vital considerations and demonstrate a broad level of knowledge and research. Some care is needed here, however. Remember to *answer the question* if it is present in the assessment. It is often the case that questions of procedure are not being asked of you. In that case do not spend time on procedure and instead focus on the liability question.

Arguably the most important trial procedures are linked to the question of the categorisation of the offence as a summary offence, indictable offence or hybrid offence. The law that applies is, of course, determined by the jurisdiction question considered at the outset. Normally that will be the jurisdiction of the court hearing the matter, and commonly the law of the state where the offence took place. The law in New South Wales as it relates to this categorisation is summarised in Table 5.1.

Table 5.1 Procedural considerations in New South Wales

Criminal Procedure Act 1986 **(NSW)**	
Section	Effect
5	Offences must be dealt with on indictment unless permitted or required to be dealt with summarily.
6(1)	Nominated offences must be dealt with summarily.
7	Summary offences to be dealt with in Local Court.
179	Summary offences must be prosecuted within 6 months of the date of the offence.
260(1)	An indictable offence listed in Table 1 (Schedule 1) is to be dealt with summarily unless the prosecution or defence elect to proceed to trial.
260(2)	An indictable offence listed in Table 2 (Schedule 1) is to be dealt with summarily unless the prosecution elect to proceed to trial.
261	If no election is made the matter is determined summarily.
267	The maximum penalty for a Table 1 offence is two years' imprisonment or 100 penalty units.
268	The maximum penalty for a Table 2 offence is two years' imprisonment or 50 penalty units.

Sentencing

In many cases the analysis ends once a conclusion is reached on the liability question. At law school that happens because word count limits will shape the extent of discussion, and sentencing is often not requested in the analysis (the task is often concerned with an appraisal of analytical skill). However, this is an artificial end to the analysis that falls short of the kind of thinking needed in practice. Practitioners and clients are *always* thinking about the consequence of conviction. Indeed, in practice the vast majority of cases going before the courts result in a finding or plea of guilt – with a significant amount of time spent on a plea in mitigation.

With that in mind, a thorough analysis will be mindful of the potential sentencing issue(s) that arise in the particular scenario. These are numerous and complex. At the very minimum, you will need to be mindful of the maximum statutory penalties, the subjective and objective features of the crime, as well as mitigating and aggravating factors that will influence the penalty. The law of sentencing is a complex area, informed by both legislation and voluminous case law.[10] The extent to which you discuss and analyse sentencing is very much determined by the nature of the task. In some cases sentencing is a major part of the exercise, while in other cases it is a minimal consideration. Be guided by the task and the nature of the problem. Where the task is primarily concerned with a liability question, then that is where the weight of discussion should be.

10 For example, in New South Wales pt 3 of the *Crimes (Sentencing Procedure) Act 1999* (NSW) will form a major part of the analysis, which directs attention to the subjective and objective aspects of the offender and the crime in the sentencing process.

When the task is primarily concerned with the outcome, then sentencing and orders (in civil matters) should be considered more heavily.

Tentative conclusion

Once you have gone through these various, more detailed stages, you will have some idea of the potential outcome(s). It becomes necessary, then, to write it up. It is likely you have already made notes and collated a good deal of information by the time you are in a position to suggest conclusions. For some this will be in the form of notes or dot points, while others will have collected a large amount of information.

The writing-up stage is tricky, as you must balance the needs of the problem with the needs of the task. If you only have 1000 words to work with, you will need to be sharp and focused. If you are a 'collector' of information, that will mean a great deal of it will have to be discarded. During the 'conclusion' stage you do not want to simply present everything you have thought about or collected, because much of it will be unnecessary. The issue is there is no capacity to engage with the content in any meaningful way, as unless you spend time getting exactly to the key issue(s), most of the information will be confusing. At the same time, if you have a larger assignment, you have a larger task ahead of you. Here the issue is often bulking up your work with waffle! In practice, you will be striking a balance between relevant information and time. Crudely stated, time is money. Clients do not appreciate being given large amounts of information if they have no direct need of it, and certainly do not like being charged for it. Think about what needs to be said. Say what needs to be said. If that requires a lengthy treatise, well and good. If not, then don't embark on that course.

Part of the art of writing conclusions and giving advice is knowing when and where to be decisive, and when and where to be tentative. Your examiners, and ultimately your clients, take comfort when clear advice is given and are less assured when your advice is equivocal or hesitant. Sometimes advice is clear and strong; other times it is necessarily equivocal. When there is a clear and direct answer to a question, then give it. Where the answer can only truly be answered by a court, this needs to be stated, with the options and range of outcomes and likely consequences also stated. The art of legal problem solving is linked to the ability to provide clarity in decision making, which is especially difficult when the facts, law and potential outcomes are uncertain. The basic rules governing these scenarios are shown in Figure 5.2.

As you can see, there are several possibilities when law and fact are combined, but in most cases the conclusion will be tentative because it will depend on the resolution of uncertain components. While this is important to understand, it is also useful to remember that in most cases the first scenario is the most common – and sometimes what you think is uncertain is actually certain; you just have not clarified the fact/law nexus at the opening stages of assessment. In the criminal context, when the facts and law are clear and unambiguous, questions of liability are rarely in issue. In such cases the most likely outcome is that the accused would be convicted if the matter went to court. In that case your advice is necessarily clear and direct. When the accused is highly likely to be convicted, a prosecutor would advise prosecuting the case, and a defendant would advise

Figure 5.2 Logic progression in problem solving

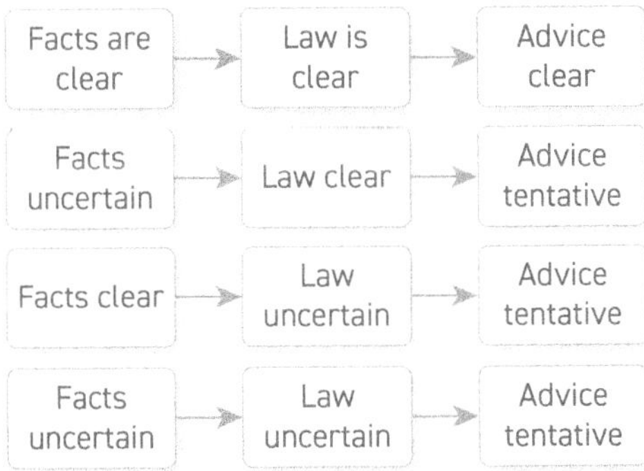

making an early guilty plea. It is not so easy where there are doubts on fact and law. Always remember that you should not be too quick to reach a conclusion. Uncertainty is a tool that should encourage you to review your work. *Always work towards a clear outcome*; but recognise that in some cases the answer will be an equivocal one. In cases where the law is unclear, it is often the case that judicial intervention will be required. In these harder cases, your conclusion may adopt a binary model like this: *If a judge decides that X is correct, then the outcome is Y. If X is not accepted by the court, then the outcome is Z.*

RECOMMENDED READING

Each of the following books contains one or more chapters on basic legal problem solving.

John Anderson, *Criminal Law Guidebook* (Oxford University Press, 2nd ed, 2016).

Michael Brogan and David Spencer, *Becoming a Lawyer: Success at Law School* (Oxford University Press, 3rd ed, 2014).

Mark Findlay, *Criminal Law: Problems in Context* (Oxford University Press, 2nd ed, 2006).

Patrick Keyzer, *Legal Problem Solving: A Guide for Law Students* (LexisNexis Butterworths, 2nd ed, 2003).

SI Strong, *How to Write Law Essays and Exams* (Oxford University Press, 5th ed, 2018).

John Wade, 'Meet MIRAT: Legal Reasoning Fragmented into Learnable Chunks' (1991) 2(1) *Legal Education Review* 283.

Bobette Wolski, *Skills, Ethics and Values for Legal Practice* (Thomson Reuters, 2nd ed, 2008).

6 PUTTING IT ALL TOGETHER

In this chapter the aim is to undertake something of a guided analysis of a problem and apply the principles discussed so far. To that end, let's now study the hypothetical example problem set out in Appendix A. For this exercise, it is useful to begin by making notes, both of the information within the hypothetical and of the law. This will require a flexible approach and access to authoritative sources. Students of the digital age are encouraged to prefer authoritative texts and professional databases for their research rather than relying on simple word searches in web browsers. Using the steps explored in the last chapter as a guide, begin by reading the hypothetical in Appendix A. Note the people involved, the event(s) and especially the question you have been asked. Make some notes on your initial thoughts, before looking back over the Chapter 5 context. Then, begin a systematic examination of the information.

Apply law to facts, or facts to law?

In this example you are assumed to be working for Legal Aid, representing your client Eric McNamara. You are advised that Eric is in possession of a court attendance notice ('CAN') that charges him with assault occasioning grievous bodily harm ('GBH'). As discussed in Chapter 2, there are normally two orientations to the law: the applicable law is either specified in the briefing, or it is not. At this stage we know the preferred charge, but not the details required by the law. In this case a useful beginning is understanding the law, which will alert us to what is important in the fact matrix.

Jurisdiction

The facts don't tell us exactly what law is in play. That is artificial, because a court attendance notice or summons would state the charge(s), the relevant law, the court and the state in which the offence is being prosecuted. The absence of references to specific law can be assumed to be part of the task set by the examiner. Where the law is not specified, the exercise will involve thinking through the nature of the cause of action, what courts operate where and for what purpose, and whether the facts indicate there are any special jurisdictional matters. The task is concerned with a form of deductive reasoning that aims to establish the existence of certain premises supporting a conclusion. As a threshold question, we need to think about what body of law is going to apply, the court in which the case will be considered, and the subject to whom to law will be applied. In this case the facts clearly indicate the offence took place in New

South Wales, that Eric has a court attendance notice, and that he has been charged with causing GBH. From that you will know the most likely offence will be located in the *Crimes Act 1900* (NSW), and likely considered in either the District or Local Courts in New South Wales. There is no clear idea of Eric's age, but since the offence took place in a hotel, we can safely assume that he is 18 years or over (although that's not absolute).

What law applies?

A consideration of jurisdiction quickly points us towards the law most likely to apply in this case, which we can assume is the criminal law of New South Wales as there is a geographic nexus between the event and the law.[1] A judicial officer would take 'judicial notice' of this.[2] As there is nothing to suggest that Commonwealth law is in play, the laws of New South Wales apply. Our general knowledge of the criminal law tells us that in New South Wales most offences against the person are located in the *Crimes Act*. We also know that most criminal procedure is regulated by the *Criminal Procedure Act 1986* (NSW); that police powers are largely regulated by the *Law Enforcement (Powers and Responsibilities) Act 2002* (NSW); and that sentencing is a hybrid of common law and provisions found in the *Crimes (Sentencing Procedure) Act 1999* (NSW). These four statutes will likely provide the primary sources of law for the analysis of this problem.

Age and state of mind

Next, we might think about whether any special law applies to Eric, so we proceed to consider legal personality. As noted above, the facts do not tell us the age of the accused, but given the offence took place in a bar, we may safely assume the accused is 18 years of age (and certainly over 14), and accordingly adult criminal responsibility applies.[3] That would indicate that normal criminal court processes apply. We are, of course, making an assumption, so here you might note that confirmation of Eric's age will be useful as it could affect the nature of proceedings if he is under 18 years of age. Here we encounter our first area of law already outside the initial scope of the initial appraisal. Technically, the Children's Court has jurisdiction over matters committed by a 'child', defined as a person under the age of 18 years. To confirm this we would want to confirm the assumption.[4] There is no evidence of mental illness or some other abnormality of mind, but there *is* evidence of intoxication in the facts. That will need to be considered in more detail in due course.

This initial appraisal positions us to start moving towards a specific offence.

1 *Crimes Act 1900* (NSW) s 10A.
2 Judicial notice is a process where a judge can 'take notice' of matters of law or factual common knowledge without formal proof being presented to the court. See, eg, *Evidence Act 1995* (NSW) ss 143, 144.
3 *Children (Criminal Proceedings) Act 1987* (NSW) s 10. At common law there is a rebuttable presumption of doli incapax between the ages of 10 and 14: see *BP; SW* [2006] NSWCCA 172; *R v CRH* (Unreported, NSWCCA, 18/12/96); *RP v The Queen* [2016] HCA 53.
4 *Children (Criminal Proceedings) Act 1987* (NSW) ss 4, 28.

Identify the harms and procedures

The opening paragraph of the facts sheet states that Eric 'assaulted Floyd Jammal at Newcastle in the State of New South Wales, and recklessly caused grievous bodily harm'. It is not entirely clear whether these are two distinct offences.

Start simply. The first step is to establish a basic understanding of these terms as a matter of law. Here we are dealing with a category of harm linked to an offence of physical violence not involving death. Some general reading of a standard chapter in a reputable textbook would be an excellent place to begin. Further, you might consider an examination of the definitions of 'assault' and 'grievous bodily harm' in one or more legal dictionaries. This initial step will not only point you towards specific law on the topic, but also alert you to specific pieces of information to look for in the facts. In your notes record the relevant quotes from your sources (always prefer authoritative primary sources, not just a simple internet search), and ensure you record the source. This may or may not be integrated into the final write-up. At this stage we are just getting a sense of the facts that will point us towards the precise law.

For example, for this task I would begin with a simple dictionary meaning of 'assault' and 'grievous bodily harm',[5] refer to (at least) two major textbook chapters on offences against the person/assaults,[6] and then look at encyclopaedic legal dictionaries,[7] combined with annotated legislation.[8]

A preliminary survey of the law indicates that 'grievous bodily harm' is a serious injury that includes 'any permanent or serious disfiguring of the person'. On its own, the fact Floyd suffered that injury does not make Eric responsible for it. There must be some connection between some act or omission of the accused that causes some physical injury.[9] This gives us some focus in reviewing the facts.

The 'harm' in our case comes in the form of the medical evidence/documents forming part of the hypothetical. It consists of 'extensive bruising and abrasions to Floyd's hands, arms, upper body and face'. We also know he was 'treated for a dislocated jaw'. We also have evidence of subsequent anxiety and fear in public places, suggesting psychological injury, with a long-term effect in the form of being unable to study or work. These injuries are directly linked to the physical altercation between Eric and Floyd.

On these facts, we also know that Eric was arrested at the scene, and that there is CCTV evidence that captures him at the scene, engaging in a fight with the victim. The identity

5 My dictionaries of choice are the *Oxford English Dictionary* and the *Macquarie Dictionary*.

6 This will depend on the jurisdiction. For New South Wales I start off with David Brown et al, *Criminal Laws: Materials and Commentary on Criminal Law and Process of New South Wales* (Federation Press, 7th ed, 2020); and Simon Bronitt and Bernadette McSherry, *Principles of Criminal Law* (Thomson Reuters, 4th ed, 2017).

7 Thomson Reuters' *The Laws of Australia* (Lawbook Co., 2012);, and Mirko Bagaric, *Ross on Crime* (Thomson Reuters, 9th ed, 2021) are favourites.

8 For example, Roderick Howie and Peter Johnson, *Annotated Criminal Legislation New South Wales* (Lexis Nexis, 2023–24).

9 *Crimes Act 1900* (NSW) s 4(1); *Haoui v R* [2008] NSWCCA; *Swan v R* [2016] NSWCCA 79. See also *DPP v Smith* [1961] AC 290.

of the accused is fundamental in crime, and as there is no issue with the identity of the accused, this aspect of liability and evidence need not be explored.[10] As an aside, most criminal law courses are taught before students study evidence, but it is important for you to know that identification forms an essential part of liability questions, and that a good deal of evidence law revolves around the rules controlling the nature and admissibility of identification.[11]

Combined, these two aspects tend to confirm that Eric has been properly charged. However, at this point we are a long way from a definitive analysis. This initial step served the purpose of confirming the direction for the analysis. If we had not been advised at all on the charge(s), this step would have narrowed down the field of enquiry. Specifics are now required.

Scope the law

During the initial scoping exercise on assault and GBH in New South Wales, you will ascertain that such offences are prohibited by pt 3 of the *Crimes Act 1900* (NSW). You will quickly work out that the most common of these are stated in ss 33 and 35. The problem we face is the scenario provided is not specific – a typical problem in a hypothetical, as part of the assessment often involves inviting the student to think about the problem and exercise judgement in the analysis. As it happens, these charges are linked, so the problem is not a critical one. But it does require an examination of both to identify the elements of the offences in the next step of the analytical process. In terms of what provisions you should prefer, be guided by the principle that *you should choose the most serious offence that the facts and the law will support.* It does not matter at this stage if you are wrong. What's important is to have a range of possibilities that are broadly aligned to the fact matrix.

Now, we have an initial starting point for a more detailed analysis. Examination of the *Crimes Act* suggests a viable starting point to be either s 33(1) or s 35(2) of the Act. Our basic question is this: *Is Eric liable for a charge under s 33(1) or 35(2) of the Crimes Act?* But as we will see, this is not the end of the story. We also need to consider a range of alternatives and be particularly mindful of procedural aspects of the case, as well as 'invisible' aspects of it.

In terms of alternatives, there is no evidence of intention to kill at this stage, so we would rule out any of the attempted murder possibilities, as intention to kill is an essential element of that offence.[12] This provides the upper limit of liability for what are known as 'non-fatal offences against the person'. The most common alternative to a charge under s 35 is found in s 59, assault occasioning actual bodily harm ('ABH'). Again, note this as we will return to it when we consider the elements of the offence.

ABH would be of immediate interest for us because it is an offence that does not require specific intent and is also grounded in the existence of a certain level

10 Classically, see *Alexander v R* (1981) 145 CLR 395.
11 See, eg, *Evidence Act 1995* (NSW) pt 3.9.
12 See, eg, *Crimes Act 1900* (NSW) s 27; *Knight v R* (1992) 175 CLR 495.

of injury, which is indicated on these facts. This is a useful alternative to consider. Thinking broadly, it is helpful to go back to first principles and reflect on the main categories of criminal offences. Simply stated, these are offences concerned with prohibited conduct, actions, circumstances, omissions and results. GBH and ABH are results. An offence concerned with conduct/actions is also plausible. One such possibility is an offence known as 'affray'. This is an offence of interpersonal violence but is sometimes identified as a 'public order' offence. In New South Wales this is an offence pursuant to s 93C of the *Crimes Act*. You might also note that this offence overlaps with another offence known as 'violent disorder' in the *Summary Offences Act 1988* (NSW).[13] Novice analysts will sometimes ask 'How do you know that?'. The answer is a combination of experience and reading. Reading broadly is part of the process.

For the purposes of this exercise, we'll stick with affray.

Now we're starting to get a better sense of the possibilities here. This is an important process, because if you focus on one charge alone, you will fail to appreciate the range of options for charge negotiation, as well as live alternatives.

Identify the elements of the proposed offence

Once you have scoped the law most likely in play, it becomes necessary to identify the operative components, because these elements will become the focus of both the evidence and interpretation of law. These are critical in identifying the essential evidence necessary to determine liability and culpability, as well as identifying those areas of law that are uncertain.

The essential rule here is to be systematic. Regardless of how extensive the potential range of law is, focus on one component at a time. Break apart the complex into chunks and deal with each systematically. Here the key is to remember the fundamentals. Criminal liability depends on the existence of certain physical elements (actus reus) and fault elements (mens rea), which need to be coexistent in time and place. When you are reading legislation, or case authority, you will always be looking for the operative parts of the law linked to these components. In other words, nouns and adjectives linked to the physical and mental elements constituting the offence.

The first step in identifying the elements of an offence is to begin with the source of law and focus on the language used. For practical purposes most Australian criminal law is embodied in legislation, although there remain common law offences in some jurisdictions, in which case the focus is very much on the language of judges in decided cases. A useful adjunct to this process is to check the latest annotated legislation, if it exists in your jurisdiction, to confirm you are correct.

13 There is a related offence in s 11A of the *Summary Offences Act 1988* called 'violent disorder', but it is not presently relevant as it requires three or more offenders.

USEFUL RESOURCES: ANNOTATED LEGISLATION

Roderick Howie and Peter Johnson, *Annotated Criminal Legislation New South Wales* (LexisNexis).
Gerard Nash, *Annotated Criminal Legislation Victoria* (LexisNexis).
Soraya Ryan et al, *Carter's Criminal Law of Queensland* (LexisNexis).

> ***Crimes Act 1900* (NSW)**
>
> **33 Wounding or grievous bodily harm with intent**
>
> (1) **Intent to cause grievous bodily harm** A person who—
> - (a) wounds any person, or
> - (b) causes grievous bodily harm to any person,
>
> with intent to cause grievous bodily harm to that or any other person is guilty of an offence.
>
> Maximum penalty—Imprisonment for 25 years.
>
> (2) **Intent to resist arrest** A person who—
> - (a) wounds any person, or
> - (b) causes grievous bodily harm to any person,
>
> with intent to resist or prevent his or her (or another person's) lawful arrest or detention is guilty of an offence.
>
> Maximum penalty—Imprisonment for 25 years.
>
> (3) **Alternative verdict** If on the trial of a person charged with an offence against this section the jury is not satisfied that the offence is proven but is satisfied that the person has committed an offence against section 35, the jury may acquit the person of the offence charged and find the person guilty of an offence against section 35. The person is liable to punishment accordingly.

The first step in any assessment is to look at the source(s) of law. You are dealing with legislation. As you can see, s 33 is a composite section that contains two offence sections and an alternative verdict. We can immediately rule out s 33(2) because the event had nothing to do with an arrest. The relevant provision is s 33(1). You can see explicit references to both physical and fault elements. The physical element of this section has two limbs: one based on a 'wound', the other by 'grievous bodily harm'. In law, these are quite distinct injuries, although in fact they may overlap. The fault element is intention to cause GBH. Therefore, your elements are:

(1) causing a wound or GBH to a person
(2) intention to do so.

> ***Crimes Act 1900* (NSW)**
>
> **35 Reckless grievous bodily harm or wounding**
>
> (1) **Reckless grievous bodily harm—in company** A person who, in the company of another person or persons—

(a) causes grievous bodily harm to any person, and
(b) is reckless as to causing actual bodily harm to that or any other person,

is guilty of an offence.

Maximum penalty—Imprisonment for 14 years.

(2) **Reckless grievous bodily harm** A person who—

(a) causes grievous bodily harm to any person, and
(b) is reckless as to causing actual bodily harm to that or any other person,

is guilty of an offence.

Maximum penalty—Imprisonment for 10 years.

(3) **Reckless wounding—in company** A person who, in the company of another person or persons—

(a) wounds any person, and
(b) is reckless as to causing actual bodily harm to that or any other person,

is guilty of an offence.

Maximum penalty—Imprisonment for 10 years.

(4) **Reckless wounding** A person who—

(a) wounds any person, and
(b) is reckless as to causing actual bodily harm to that or any other person,

is guilty of an offence.

Maximum penalty—Imprisonment for 7 years.

(5) **Alternative verdict** If on the trial of a person charged with an offence against any subsection of this section the jury is not satisfied that the offence is proven but is satisfied that the person has committed an offence against any other subsection of this section (that carries a lesser maximum penalty), the jury may acquit the person of the offence charged and find the person guilty of an offence against that other subsection. The person is liable to punishment accordingly.

Section 35 is surprisingly complicated. You will note it is a five-part section, with four containing subsections for offence provisions. As with s 33, there are two limbs: one concerned with wounding, the other with GBH. The mental element is recklessness. You will also see there are two further divisions, which are aggravated forms of each offence when the offence takes place in company. The essential elements in common are:

(1) causing a wound or GBH to a person
(2) being reckless as to causing ABH
(3) being in company (circumstance of aggravation).

***Crimes Act 1900* (NSW)**

59 Assault occasioning actual bodily harm

(1) Whosoever assaults any person, and thereby occasions actual bodily harm, shall be liable to imprisonment for five years.

(2) A person is guilty of an offence under this subsection if the person commits an offence under subsection (1) in the company of another person or persons. A person convicted of an offence under this subsection is liable to imprisonment for 7 years.

By comparison with ss 33 and 35, s 59 seems straightforward. This offence has two limbs: a basic offence, and an offence in company. The operative elements are:

(1) an assault
(2) causing actual bodily harm
(3) in company (aggravating circumstance).

***Crimes Act 1900* (NSW)**

93C Affray

(1) A person who uses or threatens unlawful violence towards another and whose conduct is such as would cause a person of reasonable firmness present at the scene to fear for his or her personal safety is guilty of affray and liable to imprisonment for 10 years.

(2) If 2 or more persons use or threaten the unlawful violence, it is the conduct of them taken together that must be considered for the purposes of subsection (1).

(3) For the purposes of this section, a threat cannot be made by the use of words alone.

(4) No person of reasonable firmness need actually be, or be likely to be, present at the scene.

(5) Affray may be committed in private as well as in public places.

When you turn to s 93C, you will see this is a complex five-part section. This is partly because affray, in its original form, was an offence at common law – so to some extent the section provides something of a 'codification'[14] of the common law. The offence provision

14 Codification involves reducing law into an explicit statement and single source of law. Where a code has been enacted, or a provision codified, it has the function of excluding any further development of the law on that area through case evolution (as with common law), and requires explicit reference to legislation on that issue. We know that is the case with affray, because it was explicitly abolished as a common law offence in 2007. See *Crimes Act 1900* (NSW) s 580H and sch 3 cl 3.

is in s 93C(1). The others are procedural. Initial reading of the section will suggest it is an offence characterised only by physical elements. That is incorrect, as it needs to be read in conjunction with s 93D.

> ***Crimes Act 1900* (NSW)**
>
> **93D Mental element under sections 93B and 93C**
>
> (1) A person is guilty of riot only if the person intends to use violence or is aware that his or her conduct may be violent.
>
> (2) A person is guilty of affray only if the person intends to use or threaten violence or is aware that his or her conduct may be violent or threaten violence.
>
> (3) Subsection (1) does not affect the determination for the purposes of riot of the number of persons who use or threaten violence.

The combination of these sections gives us the following:

(1) The accused used or threatened to use unlawful violence towards another.
(2) That conduct was such that it would cause a person of 'reasonable firmness' present at the scene to fear for their safety.
(3) That conduct must have been intended, or the accused was aware their conduct may be violent.

Having ascertained the elements of the offences, it now becomes a matter of giving legal meaning to these elements.

Preliminary interpretation

The key to interpretation is being systematic and focusing on one thing at a time. Being systematic involves addressing each concept without leaving gaps, documenting your research and thinking, and informing yourself with as much detail as you need to properly understand the concept. In this step you will likely produce, research and read a lot more information than you need for the final product, whether that is a written assignment or an advice to your client – but that is normal. As you develop expertise in the field you become more efficient and knowledgeable. At this stage of the process what we are aiming for is a general review of the elements so you are in a position to engage with the task.

Section 33 Wounding or grievous bodily harm with intent

Wound or GBH?

In a common law jurisdiction like New South Wales, legislation can function to define a term exhaustively, partially, or not at all. 'Wound' is not defined in the *Crimes Act*. It is a creature of the common law. The gist of a 'wound' is some injury that penetrates the internal layer of the skin and is evidenced by flowing blood. A wound can be life-threatening, or minor in nature.[15] GBH is partially defined in the *Crimes Act*[16] and at common law. At common law it has no fixed meaning but is always concerned with injuries of a 'really serious kind'.[17] Recently authority also suggests that s 33 may refer to a single offence, as the contours of a wound and GBH are sometimes almost impossible to distinguish. Ultimately it does not matter which of the limbs apply, and there is scope for the sentencing judge to consider the totality of the injury in the assessment of sentence.[18] We therefore know that s 33(1) could be charged on the basis of a wound (s 33(1)(a)) or GBH (s 33(1) or s 33(1)(b)).

Specific intent

A charge under s 33 is an offence of 'specific intent'. That is, it is an essential element that the accused must have *intended* to inflict serious injury on the victim. There is no requirement to look at intention in these cases in a segmented way (ie the accused intended GBH at a specific moment); rather it is a question for the jury to determine, which may include a conclusion the accused had the relevant intention throughout the whole incident.[19] As a matter of law, intention has its ordinary meaning, related to the object or desire to produce a certain result through some act or omission.[20] In other words, for this offence to be made out we need to prove the offender *intended* to inflict serious injury on the victim.

Section 35 Reckless grievous bodily harm or wounding

Injuries

Section 35 shares the same elements as s 33 in relation to wounding and GBH. As we have already considered that, it is not necessary to do so again. Finding 'elements in common' is a useful strategy when working on briefings and assessment tasks, as it enables efficient consideration of sometimes complex statutory provisions. But you will note it also involves a reference to 'actual bodily harm'. This term is a creature of the common law and is not defined. Your research will establish that injuries are conceptualised on a continuum, with death at one end and mere fright at the other. Somewhere in the

15 Classic cases on wounding are *R v Smith* (1837) 8 C&P 173 and more recently *Vallance v The Queen* (1961) 108 CLR 56; *R v Shepherd* [2003] NSWCCA 351.

16 Section 4 provides: 'Grievous bodily harm includes: (a) the destruction (other than in the course of a medical procedure) of the foetus of a pregnant woman, whether or not the woman suffers any other harm, and (b) any permanent or serious disfiguring of the person, and (c) any grievous bodily disease (in which case a reference to the infliction of grievous bodily harm includes a reference to causing a person to contract a grievous bodily disease).'

17 *DPP v Smith* [1961] AC 290; *R v King* (2003) 59 NSWLR 472; *Haoui v R* [2008] NSWCCA; *Swan v R* [2016] NSWCCA 79.

18 *Bourke v R* [2010] NSWCCA 22 (especially [70]).

19 *Sharp v R* [2012] NSWCCA 134, [26]–[28].

20 See, eg, *Hyam v DPP (UK)* [1975] AC 55; *R v Moloney* [1985] AC 905; *He Kaw The v The Queen* (1985) 157 CLR 523.

middle is 'actual bodily harm', while further towards death is GBH. As a matter of law ABH refers to any physical (or psychological) injury not otherwise grievous, but 'more than transient'.[21]

In company

The element 'in company' is a combination of presence and shared purpose. Thus, it is not sufficient that a person is simply present at the scene, but there must also exist a shared understanding as to their combined involvement. When there is a shared understanding, the proximity of the participants can move beyond immediate perception of the event. The intention and purpose need not be pre-planned, as it is open to a person to join an event at the spur of the moment.[22]

The mental element

Mens rea in this section is also different. Whereas s 33 requires intention to commit serious injury, s 35 relies on the concept of recklessness. Recklessness is a term that is partially defined,[23] but characterised at common law. Broadly, recklessness can be established where the accused foresees the possibility of the consequence and proceeds regardless[24] – but this has an extended meaning by virtue of the definition in s 4A and includes intention and knowledge. So what is needed here is not explicit intention to inflict serious injury (although that will satisfy the element), but a lower threshold. If the person has actual knowledge or foresees it is probable, their actions will cause 'actual bodily harm' that will satisfy the section.

Section 59 Assault occasioning actual bodily harm

Actual bodily harm

As we have considered this element already, it is not necessary to go into further detail. We might, however, consider the case authorities on s 59 to distinguish it from ss 33 and 35. Here you will find that ABH is an offence that is based on an assault (usually a battery) that causes injury to the victim that is less than grievous.

Assault

There is no statutory definition of assault in this section, and as such we must turn to the common law. At common law there is a distinction between assault and battery. Battery involves intentional or reckless physical contact between the accused and the victim without consent, beyond the 'exigencies of everyday life'. Most authorities accept that the contact must involve both an element of force and be conducted in a manner that

21 *R v Donovan* [1934] 2 KB 498; *R v Brown* [1993] 2 WLR 556; *McIntyre v R* (2009) 198 A Crim R 549.

22 *Brougham v R* (1986) 43 SASR 187, 191; *R v Button & Griffin* [2002] NSWCCA 159, [120]; *Markou v R* [2012] NSWCCA 64, [28].

23 Section 4A of the *Crimes Act* provides: 'Recklessness: For the purposes of this Act, if an element of an offence is recklessness, that element may also be established by proof of intention or knowledge.'

24 *R v Crabbe* (1985) 156 CLR 464; *Banditt v R* (2005) 224 CLR 262.

involves a degree of anger or hostility.[25] There is clear authority that even when there is consent, those who get involved in a fight are guilty of assault if they intend to inflict bodily harm.[26] Such actions are to be contrasted with an assault, which is concerned with the apprehension of unlawful violence. There can be an assault without a battery, and vice versa.

In company

Where the offence is in company, the above principles apply.

Section 93C Affray

Affray

Affray is essentially concerned with a continuous course of conduct, based on participation of the accused in an uninterrupted melee. Thus, it is basically a fight over a period, which will involve multiple instances of intentional physical contact between two or more individuals, or threats of the same (often in the earlier stages). That course of conduct must be such that it would cause the notional ordinary person who might be present to fear for their personal safety. This is an offence basically characterised by subjective and objective components. If the court is satisfied the accused has used violence towards another, and that conduct is such that it would cause a person of reasonably firmness present to fear for their safety, then the offence is made out.[27] There is an alternative available in s 11A of the *Summary Offences Act* that relates to 'violent disorder', but that requires three or more participants, so is not presently relevant.

The mental element

The mental state required for an offence of affray is expressed in s 93D(2), which is stated as intention or awareness of violence or an associated threat of it.

Identify the evidence

The next step is to re-examine the evidence available to us, only now we are specifically interested in evidence that may satisfy or contradict the elements of the offences we have identified. It is only now that we have a better sense of the legal meaning of the elements that the 'material facts' become clearer. It is important to do this systematically. Keep in mind that the evidence you have is not only a matter for the elements of the offence – it is also relevant to the circumstances of the offence, the offender and the victim, and in this respect is vitally important for sentencing issues, and, in some cases, procedural matters.

---

25 There are innumerable cases on assault and battery. Leading authorities include *Fagan v Metropolitan Police Commissioner* [1969] 1 QB 439; *R v Phillips* [1971] ALR 740. Note: in *Boughey v R* (1986) 161 CLR 10 it was held that hostility is not essential.

26 *AG Ref (No 6) of 1980* [1981] QB 715; *R v Raabe* (1984) 14 A Crim R 381.

27 The leading authority in New South Wales is *Colosimo v DPP* [2005] NSWSC 584, which considers a line of English authorities in conjunction with s 93C.

Injuries sustained

The first thing to consider is the nature of the injury. This is going to be critical because the injury is essential to the charges being considered. Our evidence is as follows:

> Photographs from the medical file, and the accompanying medical report, showed extensive bruising and abrasions to Floyd's hands, arms, upper body and face. On presentation to Big John Hospital, Floyd was treated for a dislocated jaw. Subsequent medical reports indicate that he was in a stable condition and recovering normally, although he was consistently reporting anxiety and fear of public places as a result of the fight.
>
> Personal information confirmed that Floyd is a 23-year-old university student, who worked part time in a grocery store while attending college. He has been unable to return to work or study since the attack.

From a practice point of view, this information is very limited. However, this is all we have at the present time. On a more advanced note, this medical evidence may trigger some related issues on admissibility. Ordinarily such evidence would be authenticated and elaborated on by the relevant medical staff.

State of mind

It is always useful to ask yourself: 'What was the state of mind of the accused?'. Here you must consider the evidence. Establishing the state of mind of a person is notoriously difficult in the absence of an explicit confession. Very often the state of mind is inferred from the surrounding evidence, including things the person said and what they did. What a person says before, during or after the event can be a useful indication of their intention, knowledge or understanding of the event. In addition, as we have seen above, you can draw inferences about this from conduct, even where the person denies this is the case. Sometimes a person's denials are, frankly, unbelievable. In practice this information often comes from witnesses and interviews, in statements and interview transcripts at first instance, but subsequently in verbal testimony. In hypotheticals, there is a need for close reading of the declared facts in order to identify information that clearly demonstrates the required state of mind, or is sufficient to rationally imply that state of mind without saying so. Consider the following:

> At one point he tried to calm the situation down by saying, 'Look, mate, even I think you've had enough – why not just go home?' Eric turned his aggression towards Floyd, yelling 'It's none of your fucking business!' He then pushed his finger aggressively into Floyd's chest with sufficient force to cause him to step back. Floyd regained his footing and yelled 'Keep your hands to yourself, arsehole!' A fight then erupted.

> CCTV footage from the door area of the bar captured most of the ensuing fight. There was an exchange of blows to the head and upper body of both men. At one point Floyd managed to knock Eric to the ground. At that time it appeared that the fight was over. Floyd then backed away. Eric got back to his feet, approached the victim and punched him to the side of the head, knocking him to the ground, where he remained. Eric was grabbed by two security guards and restrained until the police arrived.
>
> ...
>
> ... He admitted to you that he drank 'at least' five schooners of beer, but that he did not feel 'particularly drunk' – and that the trigger for him getting angry was the 'smarmy' way the bar manager had refused him service.

This information says nothing about the elements of the offences as such, which is often the case. Here you are going to need to think about the state of mind of the offender, including the fact that there is evidence of intoxication. The facts indicate a heightened level of hostility. Often the key for thinking through a state of mind is self-knowledge and experience. Think about what the offender was saying and how they were acting. Poking someone in the chest is a deliberate act, especially when it involves enough force to push away another person's body. The words spoken are combative. After being knocked to the ground, the offender stood up and struck the victim in the head with a closed fist. These actions are strongly indicative of deliberate and intentional actions. The question that remains unanswered is whether the intention was to inflict serious injury. Consider the actions, the location of the punch, the language used, and so on.

We also have some evidence of drinking alcohol. This should be a flag for us to consider intoxication. As intoxication is linked to what might be regarded as a defence (technically it is not a defence, but that's another story), we will 'park' this for the moment and return to it later in the analysis.

In company

There's no evidence to indicate that the accused was involved in this incident with other people, and certainly no agreement of the same. Accordingly, there is no factual basis on which to argue or consider the offence(s) as being 'in company'. The individuals in this case were not acting in anything like a 'common purpose'. This element is absent on the facts. Accordingly, we can confidently rule that out. This is important to note because novice analysts will sometimes conclude the offender was 'in company' merely because the event took place in a public place. That assumption is wrong and needs to be avoided.

Evidence of assault

Because the criminal law uses the term 'assault' interchangeably to refer to both assault and battery, it is necessary to consider both. In this case the evidence clearly establishes a violent exchange of physical blows, in addition to some heated words. Think about the following in addition to the material considered above:

> The statement by the arresting officer, Constable Baldwin, states that he and another officer, Constable Jones, attended the Jade Garden Hotel on Hunter Street, Newcastle, at approximately 11 pm on Australia Day, in response to a call by security guards at that venue, advising that a serious fight had broken out between two patrons. When police arrived, they found that Eric had been detained by a security guard, and the victim was being treated at the scene by ambulance officers for head injuries. Police took statements from four witnesses who all stated that Eric had been drinking at the venue and was refused service by the bar manager. Eric became abusive and was asked to leave by security. He was then escorted off the premises. Eric began to argue with one of the security guards. Floyd was waiting in line to get into the bar.

We know from our initial review of the elements of assault and battery that we are looking for evidence of both apprehended violence or fear, plus physical contact, combined with some form of intention to inflict violence or cause fear. At this point we need to consider both an assault in the form of a battery, as well as assault as the apprehension of fear. There is no specific evidence in relation to the state of mind of the parties, so it will be necessary to consider the state of mind through inferences from the facts. To some extent we have already done this above. There seems to be little room for doubt in this scenario that we have the elements of both assault and battery.

Associate and evaluate the elements and the evidence

In the preceding step we began thinking about the evidence in relationship to the relevant law. This is a crucial part of the overall process. This step overlaps with the next, which is a deeper evaluation of the evidence in relationship with the law. In this step you will be thinking about the extent to which the law clearly establishes categories in which you can then evaluate the facts. Do the facts clearly fall within the conceptual boundaries established by the law as it stands? Does the evidence rationally affect the existence of a category required by the law? To what extent? What is the weight of the evidence? Is it convincing or vague? Is the law sufficiently clear to unambiguously establish the required category? Let's now consider the categories needed for liability.

Injuries

We know that GBH is a term that has a composite meaning. Relevantly, s 4 of the *Crimes Act 1900* defines GBH as including 'any permanent or serious disfiguring of the person',[28] while the common law rather loosely includes bodily injury of a 'really serious'

28 *Crimes Act 1900* (NSW) s 4.

kind.[29] The law on this subject requires the tribunal of fact to consider the nature of the injuries on a case-by-case basis. In our scenario the physical evidence is that the victim suffered:

- extensive bruising and abrasions to the hands, arms, upper body, and face
- a dislocated jaw
- ongoing psychological issues.

Initial appraisal suggests these injuries are 'healing normally'.

As discussed, the criminal law sets out a spectrum of offences where injuries are concerned, with the most important distinctions being 'grievous' and 'actual' bodily harm. The boundary between the two is not always clear. The nature of GBH is problematic because at one level the threshold of injury may be approaching a significant degree of injury, involving permanent and serious disfigurement and, in essence, life-threatening injuries. There are some early English authorities that suggest that GBH need not be life-threatening, provided the injury is a serious interference with health or comfort of the victim.[30] The term GBH is broad, and covers a range of serious injuries; but it tends to be concerned with injuries that require major medical intervention – notably fractures.[31] Recently, in *Phillips v R* [2016] NSWCCA 159, it was held that it was open to a jury to find that multiple soft tissue injuries, including a 'fractured mandible', could constitute GBH. ABH, by comparison, is a lower threshold of injury. It has been held to mean any injury calculated to interfere with the health or comfort of the victim, but need not be permanent although it must be more than transient or trifling.[32] ABH has also been held to include psychiatric injury but must extend beyond 'mere emotions'.[33]

In this case we have a variety of physical and psychological injuries present. It seems very clear that the evidence would support *at least* a finding of ABH (at the upper end of the spectrum), but in light of *Phillips*, it would seem plausible (if not likely) that the totally of injuries would support a conclusion of GBH. Thus, the element of injury is one or the other, but more likely a conclusion of GBH.

In relation to the *intention* question, we have established that this is ultimately a question of fact for the tribunal of fact, largely based on inferences drawn from the available facts. These facts indicate at the very least that Eric intended to do *some* injury to the victim. The question is whether there is any doubt as to the *extent* of the injury. Ultimately the question to be answered is whether Eric intended to do serious injury or was reckless in his state of mind.

In company

We have already established this factor is not evident on the facts. The law affirms that being 'in company' requires both physical proximity (noting that proximity is elastic) and

29 *DPP v Smith* [1961] AC 290; *R v King* (2003) 59 NSWLR 472.
30 *R v Ashman* (1858) 175 ER 638; *R v Vickers* [1957] 2 QB 664 (CCA). Cf *R v Metharam* [1961] 3 All ER 200.
31 *R v Haoui* [2008] NSWCCA 209.
32 *R v Donovan* [1934] 2 KB 498, 509; *R v McIntyre* [2009] NSWCCA 305.
33 *R v Ireland & Burnstow* [1998] AC 147; *Li v R* [2005] NSWCCA 442.

common purpose.[34] There being no evidence of either, there is no issue. That means that there is no possibility of proving this circumstance of aggravation in any charge.

Assault

A recent and clear statement of the principles of assault was stated by the NSWCCA in *R v McIntyre*:[35]

> [40] What is an assault? The traditional common law distinction between assault and battery has largely fallen away for the purpose of application of the modern law of assault. The distinction between assault and battery noted that an assault is an act which causes another person to apprehend the infliction of immediate unlawful force on his or her person, and a battery is the actual infliction of unlawful force on another person. Where the assault takes the form of a battery, what is required is an intentional touching of the victim without that person's consent and without lawful excuse.
>
> [41] A practical distinction is sometimes drawn between a physical assault (or battery assault) and psychic assault (or apprehended unlawful force assault).
>
> [42] It is not an element of the crime of assault that injury be caused to the victim. Any touching of another person, however slight, may amount to a physical assault. It has been said that the law cannot draw the line between different degrees of violence, and therefore totally prohibits the first and lowest stage of it.
>
> [43] If actual bodily harm was occasioned by an assault, then the offender is liable to conviction and sentence for a more serious offence where the occasioning of actual bodily harm is an element of the offence. In the case of a police officer victim, this offence arises under s.60(2). In the case of a victim who was not a police officer, the relevant offence is one under s.59 of the Act.

Accordingly, the core elements of assault are based on the nature of the assault being apprehended or physical in character (or both), and the intention or reckless state of mind of the accused, and are further qualified by the consequence of the assault, and the status of the victim.

In this case we are dealing with physical injuries caused by conduct of the accused. We are therefore dealing with an assault in the form of a battery. There is no issue that the accused struck the victim, and that he did so intentionally. The conduct was clearly aggressive, and based on the way the accused attacked the victim, and set upon him multiple times, it is certainly open to infer the conduct was intentional. Given the ferocity of the attacks, and the fact the blows were aimed at the head of the victim, we may also infer that Eric's intention was to inflict actual, if not serious, injuries. It is crucial to observe at this point that the requirement to prove an 'assault' relates *only* to the element of assault as required by s 59. It is *not* an element of either s 33 or s 35. But having considered this element deeply, we know we have established *at least* the availability of a charge under s 59.

34 *R v Button & Griffen* [2002] NSWCCA 159; *FP v R* [2012] NSWCCA 182; *Markou v R* [2012] NSWCCA 64.
35 *R v McIntyre* [2009] NSWCCA 305 (footnotes omitted).

The problem of consent

We know that the absence of consent is a central ingredient in any assault. In a pithy statement of principle, Abadee J in *R v Bonora* stated: 'The term assault involves the notion of want of consent. Thus, in general terms it may be said that an assault with consent is no assault at all.'[36] This suggests that a person can consent to physical violence, which some try to rely on when involved in fighting. For policy reasons the law invalidates consent where the intention of the parties is to inflict actual injury. In this case it seems clear that both parties were intending to fight one another. Arguably, that intention indicates a willingness to participate in interpersonal violence, and as such the fighting was consensual. While this may seem like an issue, it is not. Where the purpose of the consent is to purport to legitimise an assault during a fight, where the purpose of the parties is to inflict actual injuries, then the fact of consent is invalid.[37]

The affray

Flowing from the assault, we are presented with a situation where the number of blows exchanged by the parties was extensive, and over a long period of time. The leading authority on affray is *Colosimo v DPP*.[38] It was held in that case that liability for affray is based on interpretation of the specific elements in s 93C, to be read in conjunction with ss 93A and 93D. In that case, Johnson J in the NSW Supreme Court approved the ratio of Lord Bingham in *R v Smith*[39] on the construction of affray:

> [Affray] typically involves a group of people who may well be shouting, struggling, threatening, waving weapons, throwing objects, exchanging and threatening blows and so on. Again, typically it involves a continuous course of conduct, the criminal character of which depends on the general nature and effect of the conduct as a whole and not on particular incidents and events which may take place in the course of it. Where reliance is placed on such a continuous course of conduct it is not necessary for the Crown to identify and prove particular incidents. To require such proof would deprive ... the [Act] of its intended effect, and deprive law-abiding citizens of the protection which this provision intends that they should enjoy. It would be asking the impossible to require a jury of 12 men and women to be satisfied beyond reasonable doubt that each or any incident in an indiscriminate mêlée such as constitutes the typical affray was proved to the requisite standard.[40]

Accordingly, the law requires us to look at the totality of the conduct as constituting the use or threatened use of force as a key element. There is no issue that is the case on the evidence available. The accused was engaged in a sustained fight with the defendant,

36 (1994) 34 NSWLR 74, 78.

37 *Attorney-General's Reference No. 6 of 1980* [1981] QB 715; *R v Raabe* (1984) 14 A Crim R 381; *R v Vollmer & Ors* [1996] 1 VR 95; *Department of Health and Community Services v JWB (Marion's Case)* (1992) 175 CLR 218.

38 *R v Colosimo* [2005] NSWSC 645.

39 *R v Smith* [2007] EWHC 1836.

40 *R v Colosimo* [2005] NSWSC 645, [51]–[52] (footnotes omitted).

caught entirely on CCTV. There is no doubt this would demonstrate a continuous course of violent conduct necessary to satisfy the subjective physical element of the offence.

Regrettably, there is little in the way of case authority that establishes the scope of what is meant by a 'person of reasonable firmness', and equally little scholarly commentary on the meaning or scope of the term. The gist here is an objective test, determined by the tribunal of fact. *The question is whether or not it would be open for a jury to conclude that a person of reasonable firmness, present at this event, would fear for their personal safety.* On this evidence the answer is 'yes'. Police were called to the scene by local security, who clearly had difficulty in containing the ferocity of the incident. In these cases, it can be useful to consider how you, as an individual, would feel in this situation. In the ordinary course of human experience people, as a rule, do not like to be present in the face of this kind of aggression, and routinely flee, or sometimes intervene. But fear is a very common and likely reaction, and therefore it would be open to conclude that a reasonable person would fear for their safety in this situation.

The mental element for affray is defined in s 93D(2), and includes both *intention* and *awareness* of violence. Again, there seems to be no issue here. As 'intention' is concerned with directing the mind to achieve a certain result, circumstance or mobilise conduct, it seems impossible in this case that the actions of the accused are anything but intentional.

Reject the weak, embrace the strong

The evidence in this case in relation to the elements of assault and affray are unambiguous, and clearly supported by the evidence. It seems very likely that the standard of proof (beyond reasonable doubt) would be met in relation to these.

The evidence in relation to the nature of the injuries has a degree of ambiguity in it. It is not clear whether the injury would fall neatly under GBH or ABH – but there is no doubt that injury has been sustained, and that it is clearly attributable to the accused. This is not a weakness in the case but is worth considering in more detail and we will do so later. The fact the injury constitutes ABH is a conclusion we can reach with a degree of certainty. Whether it crosses the threshold for GBH is less clear.

The evidence of the state of mind of the accused must, at this stage, rely on inferences based on the conduct of the accused. In the absence of confession evidence from the accused we do not know what his state of mind was; but the inferences that are available are sufficiently strong to suggest there was intention to cause *some* injury.

There is no evidence that can support the 'in company' aspect of the law, so this must be rejected at the outset.

Overall, one of the problems in this case is linked to the factual questions about intention and the degree of injury. This is something that will have to be addressed in the conclusion.

Resolve factual uncertainties

There are two factual uncertainties evident. The first is the question of the intention of the offender. The second is the extent of injury suffered by the victim.

Uncertainties often appear to be insurmountable but need not be. Reasoning in uncertainty can be stabilised by a set of related questions. The basic question would be: Is the injury suffered by the victim GBH? As a matter of legal logic there will only be two answers: yes or no. Getting to that answer involves marshalling the evidence for and against that conclusion in light of the available case authorities and statutory definition(s). Sometimes that process will affirm your opinion, but a useful middle path if you remain in doubt is to adopt the following sub-questions: (1) *If the tribunal of fact decides the injury is GBH, what is the outcome?* (2) *If the tribunal of fact decides the injury is not GBH, what is the outcome?* This process of reasoning is represented in Figure 6.1.

Figure 6.1 Resolving ambiguities in elements of law

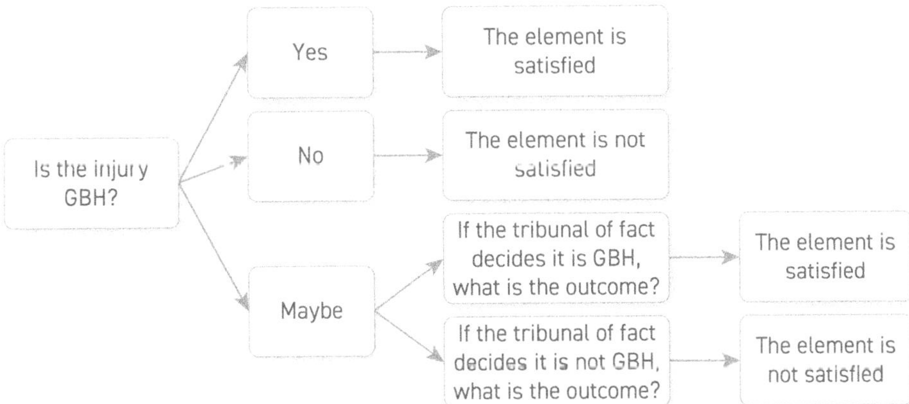

As can be seen the essential answers relate to whether or not the relevant element has been satisfied, and the consequences that flow from that. So, if we assume the tribunal of fact finds the injury *is* GBH, then that element is satisfied. Conversely, if not, then the element is not made out. In this case if the GBH element is established, then it remains for the mental element to be found. If not, then a charge under ss 33 and 35 fails because GBH is an essential element for an offence under those provisions.

The same logic can be applied to the mental elements of the offences. Is there evidence that Eric intended to inflict serious injury when he assaulted Floyd? Again, if yes, then the element is established. If not, then it is not established. And it then becomes a matter of thinking through the consequences of that outcome. If there is no evidence of specific intention, is there evidence of recklessness? If so, then this element is established. As we discussed, mental elements can be tricky because they often rely on conclusions drawn from inferences. Inferences can be drawn from the conduct and actions of the accused, but there are important limitations on the inferences available. We know from decisions such *R v Ryan*,[41] *Hodge*[42] and *Edwards*[43] (see Chapter 3) that the general

41 *R v Ryan* (Unreported, Court of Criminal Appeal, Gleeson CJ, Mahoney JA and Wood J, 15 April 1994).
42 *R v Hodge* (1838) 168 ER 1136.
43 *Edwards v The Queen* (1993) 178 CLR 193.

rule is that guilt can only be concluded where it is the only rational inference that can be drawn from the evidence. In *Ryan*, Mahoney JA reasoned:

> There are two steps in this reasoning process: is it possible to draw that inference?; and (if it is), should it be drawn in the particular case? [...]
>
> In principle, it is possible to draw that inference that X did exist if human experience has shown that in a sufficient number of cases where A has been found to exist, X will have existed. [...]
>
> If the inference is possible, it remains to be determined whether, in the circumstances of the particular case, it should be drawn. At the risk of over-refining common sense, this part of the reasoning may be described as follows. In some cases, the relationship between A and X is invariable and almost always so: whenever X exists, A will have existed. In such a case, the inference is not merely a possible one: it is proper that it be drawn in fact.[44]

So, is it possible to draw the inference that the accused, in this case, intended to assault the victim? According to Mahoney JA, that inference is open where human experience has shown us the intention to assault exists where people aggressively approach the target, and strike them with clenched fists, particularly where the area of the body is vulnerable (especially the head, neck and groin). Striking another is not, normally, an accidental event; and striking the head less so. The quick movement in the direction of the target cannot be anything other than an exercise of free will. Getting up off the ground is also an exercise in free will. Is there any other rational explanation for the conduct of the accused? It appears not. Accordingly, it is certainly possible to infer the accused intended to strike (on several occasions) the victim in this case.

The second part of the test invites us to consider whether that inference is properly made in the circumstances. The answer can only be 'yes'. It is central to liability; there is no other plausible explanation for how the accused behaved. Consequently, it appears there are solid grounds for concluding the existence of a culpable state of mind, whether it related to the required intention for a GBH charge, assault, or affray.

It gets a little tricky, however, when we start to think about the 'specific intent' necessary to convict the accused of a charge under s 33. As with all questions of fact, this is a matter for the tribunal of fact to consider. What is important here is the accused must have intended to cause serious injury. Recently in *Sharp v R* it was held that in cases involving acts of 'continuous violence', it is an error to focus on any specific action as being the direct cause of the injury, and to then focus on a state of mind at that time. Rather, the jury must consider the event in its totality, and consider whether the intention of the accused existed throughout the incident.[45] Given our consideration of the intent above as a rational inference, it would be open for a jury to make the conclusion that the accused did, in fact, intend to inflict serious injury on the victim.

44 *R v Ryan* (Unreported, Court of Criminal Appeal, Gleeson CJ, Mahoney JA and Wood J, 15 April 1994) BC9402482, 4, 5.

45 [2012] NSWCCA 134, [27].

In the absence of that finding, the alternative state of mind is found in s 35, which is concerned with the reckless infliction of actual bodily harm. Here the test for recklessness is concerned with foresight of the possibility of inflicting actual injury. It seems certain that if the jury was not satisfied that the intention was to inflict serious harm in this case, then a finding of recklessness under s 35 is highly likely. Keep in mind that in both instances there is a statutory alternative verdict that provides a default in the event of doubt.

Resolve legal uncertainties

In this case there do not appear to be any legal uncertainties. At each point of our analysis the law is clear, in both legislative and judicial sources. The one exception to this is possibly the question of a person of 'reasonable firmness'; but that seems an unlikely issue of any significance in this case. The test is clearly an objective test, and the facts of this case present a high degree of public violence very likely to be the cause of alarm and fear in the eyes of the public.

In more difficult scenarios you may be faced with legislation that presents distinct ambiguities, the most significant of which will be questions linked to the constitutionality of the legislation itself, or to drafting ambiguities. Drafting ambiguities tend to arise either in the context of very recent legislation, or where old legislation becomes subject to amendments over time. In such cases it is not unusual for conflicts to emerge between new amendments and old segments that are often anachronisms. For present purposes we can draw some comfort that is not the case here.

Defence(s)

There are two potential 'defences' that may apply in this scenario: intoxication and provocation. This is because the evidence indicates the accused had been drinking alcohol, that he claimed that he had been provoked by the 'smarmy' attitude of the barman, and the intervention of the victim as he was trying to gain entry to the bar. We must consider both.

The first issue can be dealt with quickly. Provocation is *not* a defence in the law of New South Wales except it is a partial defence to murder. It is, however, potentially relevant to sentence.[46] Accordingly, we need not examine provocation as anything more than a potential sentencing matter.

Intoxication

Intoxication is governed by pt 11A of the *Crimes Act*. It is a reference to the person being 'influenced by alcohol or drugs'.[47] We know from the evidence the accused was present at the venue for the purpose of socialising and drinking. He did so willingly and in full knowledge of what he was doing. His intoxication is 'self-induced'.[48]

46 See *Crimes Act 1900* (NSW) s 23; *Crimes (Sentencing Procedure) Act 1999* (NSW) s 21A(3)(c).
47 *Crimes Act 1900* (NSW) s 428A.
48 Ibid.

Part 11A relies on a distinction between offences of 'general' and 'specific' intent, following the English decision of *R v Majewski*,[49] and the controversial decision of the High Court in *R v O'Connor*.[50] Here an offence of 'specific intent' is defined as 'an offence of which an intention to cause a specific result is an element'.[51] Section 33 is identified as such an offence. Sections 35, 59 and 93C are not so identified. Section 428C of the *Crimes Act* permits evidence of intoxication to be used 'in determining whether the person had the intention to cause the specific result necessary for an offence of specific intent'. This is qualified, though, if there is evidence the person became intoxicated in order to commit the offence. In that case intoxication is ignored.

Accordingly, as a charge under s 33 is an offence of specific intent, it is open to consider whether or not the accused had the intention to cause the specific result – that is, an intention to inflict serious injury. So far as the other offences are concerned, evidence of self-induced intoxication cannot be considered. As the accused was drinking alcohol voluntarily, this was self-induced. Accordingly, the evidence of intoxication in this case can only be considered in respect of the s 33 charge.

While it is open to the accused to rely on intoxication, it would seem very unlikely that the level of intoxication evident on the facts would satisfy the degree of intoxication necessary in this case. The accused was clearly quite agile and aggressive in his conduct. On his own admission, he stated that he did not feel 'particularly drunk', although he had been refused service at the bar.

As there is evidence of intoxication, there is a burden on the prosecution to prove, beyond reasonable doubt, that the accused had capacity to form, and in fact formed, the relevant intention (namely, to inflict serious injury). There does appear to be a degree of uncertainty in the law on this point. In *R v Makisi* the NSW Court of Criminal Appeal drew a distinction between *capacity* and *formation* of intention.[52] The central issue is concerned with the intention, as opposed to capacity – although the terms are linked. Capacity is linked to the ability of the person to reason. Formation is concerned with the outcome of a process of thinking. In the present case there does not seem to be a serious issue. The NSW *Criminal Trial Courts Bench Book* model direction clearly advises that it is still open to the jury to find that a person may be well affected by alcohol, but still possess the relevant intention to injure another in that state. It is a matter of careful examination of the evidence.[53] In this case it would be open to the tribunal of fact to find the accused possessed the relevant intention, even with the presence of alcohol in his system.

49 [1977] AC 443.

50 (1980) 146 CLR 64. The case was controversial because it held that a person who was intoxicated may well lack the necessary mens rea to be held criminally responsible for their actions. The political and press reaction branded the decision a 'drunk's charter', although this is probably a poor reading of the actual terms of the decision.

51 *Crimes Act 1900* (NSW) s 428B(1).

52 [2004] NSWCCA 333, [12]–[13].

53 Judicial Commission of New South Wales, 'Intoxication', *Criminal Trial Courts Bench Book – Trial Instructions H–Q* (Web Page) <https://www.judcom.nsw.gov.au/publications/benchbks/criminal/intoxication.html>.

Self-defence?

In the context of brawling, the question of self-defence should always be considered. It has not been raised in this case, but it is possible that self-defence may emerge as an issue. Given, however, that the accused was, in fact, the initial aggressor, this seems unlikely. It should, however, be noted as a possible issue in any further advice provided. In New South Wales, self-defence has effectively been codified in s 418 of the *Crimes Act* and should be reviewed as part of the analysis, although, as suggested, the facts do not appear to support it. As an exercise review that section and then apply it to the facts to assess whether this conclusion is a reasonable one.

Alternatives

Statutory alternative verdict

The question of alternative outcomes arises out of a combination of facts and law. In this case we have statutory alternative verdicts, represented by the division between ss 33 and 35. The latter is a statutory alternative to the former in every case. If the jury is not satisfied the accused possessed the relevant specific intention, then it may convict the accused under s 35.

Alternative charges

A charge pursuant to s 59 does appear to be open on the facts and the law. It would require, however, a conscious decision on the part of the prosecutor to charge the offence as an alternative in the pleadings as there is no statutory verdict available.

The charge of affray is a separate and stand-alone charge that overlaps with the assault. We have established this charge may be available when the facts and law are considered.

It would seem that we have three paths in the current set of facts:

(1) The accused may be liable for charges linked to causing GBH.
   (a) Here the relevant charge appears to be one of intentionally inflicting GBH pursuant to s 33 of the *Crimes Act*.
   (b) The fact there is a statutory alternative verdict available to default to s 35 is a useful prosecution aid as the question of *intention* is likely to be at issue.
(2) An alternative charge is one count of assault occasioning ABH.
   (a) That alternative arises to cater for the question of the severity of the injury. If not satisfied the injury is GBH, this is a suitable 'back up' available under s 59 of the *Crimes Act*.
(3) The final possibility is a single count of affray pursuant to s 93C of the *Crimes Act*.
   (a) This charge is useful because (i) it does not rely on the severity of any injury, and (ii) the penalty range is sufficient to capture the seriousness of the offending.

Beware double jeopardy

When thinking about prosecution we need to be wary of 'double jeopardy'. Double jeopardy is a broad expression that refers to being punished or prosecuted twice for the same thing. It arises in cases where a person is on trial for (or being punished for) the same set of facts.[54] This is impermissible as a matter of law. For practical purposes claims of double jeopardy can operate as a plea in bar of prosecution or conviction but can also arise where aggravating or mitigating factors forming part of the elements of the offence are factored into sentencing.[55] The problem here is rather 'murky', because a factual scenario may be such that it can be broken into discrete events and pursued as such. Thus, if there was a discernable break in the sequence of events, then two distinct paths may be open. Practically speaking, this is ill-advised, because it imports into the case a clear point of appeal and legal complexity in an otherwise clear case. For that reason, it would be preferable to approach the case in a manner that is best supported by settled law and clear facts. In this context you should always consider the most serious charge(s) that the law and available facts will support as being in the scope of the analysis.

The other major choice raised in this case is whether it will be determined summarily or on indictment. Much depends on the ultimate charge to be pursued; but given that s 33 appears to be available on the facts, and there is a live issue as to whether it constitutes GBH, it seems very likely this matter would proceed to trial as either a strictly indictable offence, or on the exercise of the discretion of the prosecution as either Table 1 or Table 2 offences. Prosecution decisions must, of course, be made in conjunction with the prosecution guidelines,[56] but it would seem unlikely, given the nature of the injuries, the gravity of the offending and the nature of the likely charges that the matter would be dealt with summarily. But this is a question that can only be answered by looking in detail at the related procedural matters.

Procedural considerations

Fundamentally important procedural aspects of your advice are hidden. For many students the 'hidden' components of a task are the most troublesome, because unless you are advised about them, or undertake exhaustive research, you don't know what you don't know. Such matters are reflected in important gaps in reasoning. Procedural matters can be divided into pre-trial, trial and post-trial phases of the criminal justice process. Each phase has different governing law, reflected in Figure 6.2.

In the present scenario, there is no indication of any matters linked to police process. At this point there is a real risk of delving into a vast amount of content that has no present relevance to the task. Our inquiry is very much concerned with criminal liability questions. We will therefore confine the analysis to two areas that apply in all cases:

54 See *Pearce v The Queen* (1998) 194 CLR 610; *Island Maritime Limited v Fillipowski* (2006) 226 CLR 328.

55 *Connelly v DPP* [1964] AC 1254.

56 New South Wales Office of the Director of Public Prosecutions, 'Prosecution Guidelines' (Web Page) <http://www.odpp.nsw.gov.au/prosecution-guidelines>.

Figure 6.2 The phases of the criminal justice process

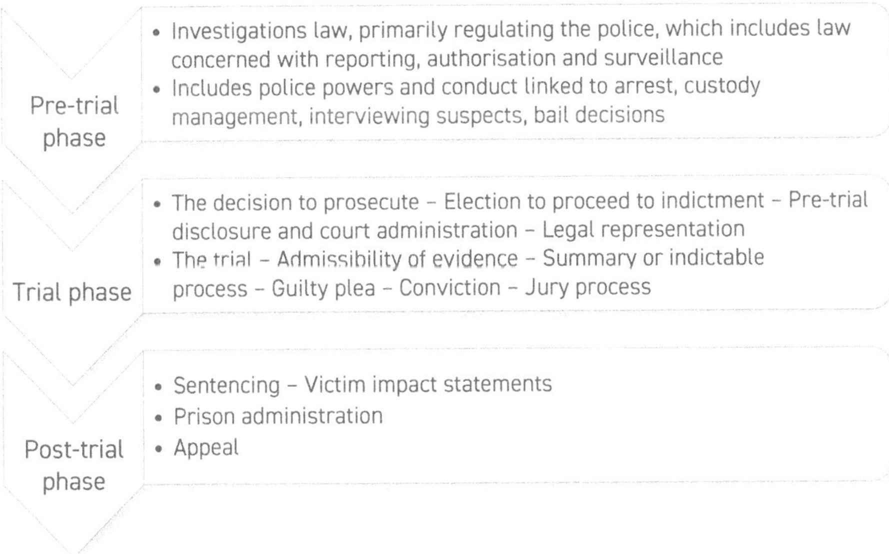

(1) whether any limitation period applies to the charge, and (2) whether the offences in our scenario are indictable or summary in their nature. These are related questions. This has critically important consequences, both in terms of what court the matter is considered in, and the maximum penalties that apply.

Limitation periods?

This can be dealt with quickly. These charges are all indictable. No limitation period applies. There is nothing to consider further.

Indictable or hybrid offences?

In New South Wales, the *Criminal Procedure Act* contains provisions that apply to all matters heard in criminal courts, but the extent of that application will vary according to the nature of the case. Table 6.1 provides a summary of the relevant provisions.

We must consult Tables 1 and 2 in the Schedule to ascertain the nature of the charges identified. In this case we have identified ss 33(1), 35(1), 59 and 93C as likely. On review of the *Criminal Procedure Act*, what you will find is the following:

- *Section 33* (Intentional infliction of GBH) is not in the Schedule. This is not surprising. Given the penalty here is a maximum of 25 years, this is a 'strictly indictable offence', which means it must proceed to a jury trial. That means the matter would be referred to the DPP by the police for prosecution.[57]

57 See *Director of Public Prosecutions Act 1987* (NSW) pt 3.

Table 6.1 Summary of relevant provisions in the *Criminal Procedure Act 1986* (NSW)

***Criminal Procedure Act 1986* (NSW)**	
Section	Effect
5	Offences must be dealt with on indictment unless permitted or required to be dealt with summarily.
6(1)	Nominated offences must be dealt with summarily.
7	Summary offences are to be dealt with in Local Court.
179	Summary offences must be prosecuted within 6 months of the date of the offence.
260(1)	An indictable offence listed in Table 1 (Schedule 1) is to be dealt with summarily unless the prosecution or defence elect to proceed to trial.
260(2)	An indictable offence listed in Table 2 (Schedule 1) is to be dealt with summarily unless the prosecution elect to proceed to trial.
261	If no election is made the matter is determined summarily.
262	If an election is made, the trial process is engaged.
263	The time for making an election is set by the court.
264	Procedure for withdrawing election.
267	The maximum penalty for a Table 1 offence is two years' imprisonment or 100 penalty units.
268	The maximum penalty for a Table 2 offence is two years' imprisonment or 50 penalty units.

- *Sections 35 and 93C* (Reckless infliction of GBH) are Table 1 offences. Such matters are dealt with summarily *unless* the prosecution or the defence make an election to proceed on indictment to trial.
- *Section 59* (Assault causing ABH) is a Table 2 offence. These matters are dealt with summarily *unless* the prosecution makes an election to proceed on indictment to trial.

We are now in a position to make an evaluation. All the charges are indictable. However, only s 33 is strictly indictable, meaning that a great deal depends on decisions made by the prosecutor on what charge is preferred. From the defendant's point of view, it is strategically important that the matter is heard in the Local Court, rather than proceeding to trial. The reason for that is linked to the fact that there is a jurisdictional limit on the penalties that can be ordered by the Local Court. The prosecution, on the other hand, is duty bound to prosecute cases in ways that properly reflect the offending. In this case given the gravity of the injuries, it seems highly likely this matter will proceed as an indictable offence.

Sentencing

The end phase of the analysis would consider questions of penalty and sentencing. As discussed, sentencing is a highly complex and nuanced body of law, and fundamentally governed by the discretion of the judicial officer. Much depends not only on the offences charged, but also on the subjective and objective aspects of the case, as well as what the accused does in the wake of any charges. As mentioned in the last chapter, many introductory criminal law courses do not make a detailed treatment of sentencing. In practice, sentencing (at least in indictable matters) is usually briefed to counsel. Novice analysts should, however, be mindful of the basis in any opening analysis of liability.

For our purposes it is enough to outline the following:

(1) The maximum penalties that apply in this case are:
  (a) intentionally causing GBH: 25 years
  (b) reckless infliction of GBH (s 35(2)): 10 years
  (c) assault occasioning ABH (s 59): 5 years
  (d) affray: 10 years.
(2) These penalties are affected by the choice of venue. If the matter is dealt with summarily, rather than on indictment, then the penalty will be capped at two years.
(3) In New South Wales, sentencing is affected by a number of statutory considerations found in the *Crimes (Sentencing Procedure) Act 1999* (NSW). The most important of these are noted below.
  (a) Whether the accused pleads guilty to the charges. If so, depending on the timing of the plea, the accused will be entitled to a statutory discount on the sentence, which may be as high as 25 per cent (s 22; *R v Thomson & Houlton* (2000) 49 NSWLR 383).
  (b) Whether the court has taken an active case management role throughout the committal process (pt 3).
  (c) The court is required to consider factors that may aggravate the assessment of culpability (s 21A(2)), including (relevantly):
    (i) The offence involved actual violence (s 21A(2)(b)).
    (ii) The injury/harm was substantial (s 21(2)(g)).
  (d) The court is required to consider factors that may mitigate the assessment of culpability (s 21A(2)), including (relevantly):
    (i) The offence was not orchestrated or planned (s 21A(3)(b)).
    (ii) The offender was provoked (s 21A(3)(c)).
    (iii) The offender has good prospects of rehabilitation (s 21(3)(h)).
  (e) If the accused demonstrates genuine remorse, this may be relevant (s 21A(3)(i)).
(4) The issue of provocation cannot reasonably be entertained on these facts.
(5) The fact the accused has five prior convictions for assault in very similar circumstances is problematic.

Tentative conclusion

Now, it appears there are three possibilities.

Option 1: The accused is liable for a charge of intentionally causing GBH pursuant to s 33 of the *Crimes Act*

In the event there is doubt as to the state of mind of the accused, s 35 provides a statutory alterative. To ensure that criminality is captured, it would be advisable to also consider s 59 as a specific alternative charge.

This option has several advantages. It confines the legal and factual challenges to specific elements that are supportable on the facts and the law. It also rests upon evidence that appears to be very strong, with only marginal variations in the conclusions of fact. There seems to be no doubt as to the physical elements; and only marginal doubt as to the mental element – but even here it seems like there is a strong prosecution case.

The disadvantage with this approach is that the prosecution case relies on two elements that will be contested: (1) the characterisation of the injury as 'grievous' and (2) the *intention* of the offender. That may result in the GBH charge(s) failing.

Option 2: The accused is liable for affray, pursuant to s 93C of the *Crimes Act*

This option has an important advantage over option 1, and that is the elements of the offence are easy to prove, and do not rely on sophisticated or nuanced examination of intention to cause any particular injury or arguments about the characterisation of injury. The problem with this approach is that it does not seem to adequately account for the very serious nature of the injury caused. Arguably, the fact the affray caused serious injury would place the sentence of this case at the upper range of seriousness; given the penalty that applies here is less than half the maximum for a charge under s 33, it seems that this option really understates the criminality involved. Given the prosecution must consider the interests of the victim in the prosecution calculation, it seems that although option 2 is viable, it really lacks sufficient weight to pursue in the public interest.

Option 3: The accused is liable for both sets of charges

As discussed above, the problem with option 3 is that it imports a field of contestation as to liability in the form of the complex area of law known as double jeopardy. Pursuing this line of inquiry would invite a highly refined scrutiny of the facts and should therefore be avoided. In addition, it is incumbent on the prosecution of criminal cases that the accused is not unfairly exposed to prosecution and punishment in the process of justice. We would therefore advise against option 3.

WRITING IT UP

7

Writing up your answer is shaped by context. As a student, you are often called upon to answer a problem question in a specific format, such as a memorandum or letter of advice, with the added complication of a word limit. Students are often not aware that the requirement for them to write in a particular manner, with specific limits, is a pedagogical tool intended to reflect the kinds of documents used in practice, along with the need to strike a balance between accuracy and brevity. Being able to write sharply is an important skill in practice. Practitioners are also restricted by context. There is simply no point in writing a treatise on the law to an unsophisticated client. Most of it would not be understood. Even sophisticated clients will not appreciate lengthy analysis if it is not necessary, or has not been asked for. Advice writing is time consuming and costly. Detailed analysis is a skill that a practitioner needs to have, but need not deploy in every case. The most likely case for lengthy analysis is in the context of written submissions on a point of law, pre-trial summaries or scholarly articles. But even in these contexts there will be restrictions.

By now you should have a sense that the legal process is a complex one, and part of the art of lawyering is being able to translate complexity so that different audiences can understand a particular situation. A person without legal training should have things explained as simply as possible. A practitioner will need the essential detail, but keep in mind that time is money, and verbose correspondence is unnecessary and not appreciated. A barrister should have all the relevant information presented in such a way that the issues and complexities are clear and sharply identified, but with sufficient detail to be able to do the required research and advice as needed. Submissions made to a court will require relevant information necessary to make a legally informed decision, especially where an appeal on a question of law is concerned.

Purpose and audience

A useful place to start is to think about your audience. Who are you writing for? What level of knowledge of the law do they have? What is the purpose of the document?

Defendants in criminal matters are usually concerned with two questions: (1) will they be convicted?; and (2) are they going to prison? Prosecutors are routinely concerned with establishing a case strong enough to secure a conviction and ensuring the penalty is proportionate to the crime. Counsel for either side will require more detailed information on the evidence, the law and any instructions: are they required to appear, advise on law, advise on evidence? In civil cases, the client is often concerned with the prospects of success, the costs involved and the presentation of options. Remember, part of the purpose of writing an advice is to enable your client to properly understand the situation and their options in order to make informed decisions that directly affect personal interests. The core message here is that your writing needs to be guided by your purpose.

In the context of writing for law school assignment, your purpose is to answer the question and to demonstrate a set of competencies. Those competencies will include a command of the relevant law, the demonstration of reasoning skill and the demonstration of professional writing. When at law school your task is often to address two things: (1) your knowledge of the subject and (2) your ability to convey it to a tertiary standard. One of the core distinctions between student writing and professional writing is that the professional is often required to demonstrate knowledge and understanding of the law in its relationship to the facts – that is assumed for the lawyer writing professionally. In the educational context the student will usually need to explain the law in more detail than they would in the professional context, although that will depend on the circumstances. There is overlap between educative and professional writing, especially in hard cases that may require addressing a question of law.

Format

There is an infinite variety of combinations of written responses to questions asked about the law, at least in terms of *format*. There is no single standard, except where the courts direct that documents be set in prescribed form, or employers require their legal staff to write in accordance with certain templates. Over time the legal profession has evolved various precedent documents and forms, so there are areas in legal work in which there is a good degree of consistency. But in all cases, what is of fundamental importance in legal writing is a combination of principles linked to mastery of written expression. Modern law, above all things, is linked to an advanced command of language. That means that lawyers *must* be able to write, read and comprehend language at a standard well beyond basic literacy. Not only that, but the level of mastery *must* be broad enough to translate the complex to the simple, and back again.

A great deal has been written about the art of legal writing. Further reading on this topic is set out at the end of the chapter. For what it is worth, below I present a set of principles that I have found useful in writing practice.

A key requirement is *order*. The document needs to be orderly in that its format needs to be clear and consistent. Remember, you are writing something that is going to be read by someone who wants information. What the reader does *not* want is to be battling with the document. Where possible, you should use fully justified paragraphs with consistent margins. Make use of headings and subheadings, especially when there are complex issues. Numbering of paragraphs is also useful because it assists the reader in discussing the document with you, and others, at a later stage. Always keep in mind that the document you are writing is *personal*. It has your name on it. At law school the document is being submitted to those who will assess it. In professional life, the document is being submitted to a person or organisation that will rely on it. In addition, in the digital age you should assume that everything you write is *permanent*. Documents invariably will be stored and are retrievable. They can be instantly communicated, replicated and modified. One of the burdens of professional life is the knowledge and duty of putting your name to a document with legal consequence. Keep that in mind at all times.

Attend to the writing process

Simply stated, the writing needs to be *impeccable*. That means the spelling, grammar and sentence construction must be 100 per cent correct. Or, at the very least, aim for that. Even seasoned writers make mistakes, which can arise through simple typographic errors, using dictation software, fatigue, and sometimes simple error. None of us are perfect. But the difference between an expert and a novice is knowing that, and taking steps to correct it. If you expect errors, you are more likely to proofread and edit. But when you are rushed, or simply unaware, it is far more likely you will write a document that other people will 'battle' with. Your reader does not want to be 'battling' with the document. That state of mind happens when the format of the document is confusing and certainly when the writing is poor. Language matters. It is surprising the number of law students whose writing skills are lacking. There is nothing so disappointing as a lawyer than receiving correspondence in which the author does not know the difference between 'there', 'they're' and 'their'; cannot use an apostrophe; or uses 'cort' for 'court'. In law, correspondence is a *critical* part of professional life. Documents will carry your signature. Your written work is a reflection of your professionalism. You should operate on the principle that everything you write could end up in a court, being scrutinised by senior members of the legal profession. It is simply not good enough in a profession in which language is the fundamental tool of the trade to write at a standard anything less than a tertiary standard. The elegance of language is *entirely* in the hands of the author. There is no excuse for not getting that part of the document right. You should consider the impact of submitting poorly written documents to a court, your client, and other professionals. In the worst-case scenario, you may find yourself sanctioned for unsatisfactory professional conduct, or sued for professional negligence. In the student context, that low standard would translate into poor marks. There is a fundamental link between written expression, demonstrated understanding, comprehension, and ability to explain and apply the law. While writing is a learned skill, it has two aspects that are often overlooked by student lawyers.

First, there is the *foundation*. It is assumed that someone who enrols at university possesses a level of literacy sufficient to engage with the complexities of higher education. And yet we live in an age when few people under the age of 20 have ever written a letter or read a book that was not set as required reading at school – and even then, it is normal for a student to look up a summary on the internet or watch a movie of the book, rather than take the time to read. The digital age has produced a generation of people who don't read or write anything like their predecessors. Indeed, I have observed numerous times in my career students routinely *not* reading cases or textbooks, and instead relying on shared notes, summaries, and YouTube videos. They wonder why their written work is so poor! It is because these students are not immersed in the practices of reading and writing in the years leading up to university.

Second, there is the *practice*. It is very common for students to regard their assessments at university as going through a production line. They are taught to submit products at certain dates. What they are often not taught is that the product is the result of a *process*. In writing, students tend to think of the document they submit as the product. That is partially true – but in most cases that submitted product is incomplete because it has not been properly constructed and processed. A typical student approach to writing involves timetabling assignment due dates and starting the work a few days before it is due. What then follows is 8–12 hours assigned to research (if that), usually wholly electronic, spread across two days. The writing is often done at the same time, usually consisting of a collection of whatever research was retrieved at first instance. The result is a document the student has collected without actually knowing the topic they are writing about. The final product is submitted on the due date – usually in the hour before it is due. *What many submit, in effect, is the first draft.*

This practice is obvious to examiners. We see it all the time. Indeed, with the various databases used for submission, it is possible to know the exact point in time at which the document was submitted. The metadata on the document clearly shows the trail of where the document was prepared, and the time spent on it. The real joy is when the student is then marked on that paper, and the student then gets cranky because the result is poor. Simply stated, you are responsible for the result, not the examiner.

A better strategy is to factor in *drafting* and *editing* as a central part of the process. The first draft is rarely submission-ready. It is better that you proofread the first draft with a red pen, read through it aloud, and make corrections. If it sounds awkward, it probably is. Correct spelling mistakes. Check punctuation use and sentence construction. If you are unsure about grammar and writing essentials, *research them.* There are several excellent references to keep handy as you write.[1] Ideally, you should write your assessments *at least* three clear days before they are due. Leave them overnight, and then engage in the corrections. When necessary, redraft the paper. By doing this you are more likely to submit a better product because you are engaging in the process. But even before you begin writing, you should spend some time reading and researching the topic so you actually know something about what you are writing about. Confidence in writing comes from understanding enough of the topic to be able to write about it. Work out the important authors, the nature of the task and problem, and spend some time planning the document before you write it. You will have seen in the preceding chapters that a large part of the process involves mapping out what you're going to say, before you say it.

Engage with the law

By far the most common error in legal writing (outside the writing) is the failure of students to engage with the *law.* That happens because the student has not done enough reading to know, and then recognise, what the *legal issues* are. The result is a tendency to focus on the facts of the case, and then engage in a largely fact-focused and common-sense description involving rudimentary law associated with a reinterpretation of the facts. And because the student does not know what they don't know, it often comes as a shock when the mark is returned.

1 For example, Henry Fowler, *Fowler's Dictionary of Modern English Usage* (Oxford University Press, 2015); Michael Meehan and Graham Tulloch, *Grammar for Lawyers* (LexisNexis Butterworths, 3rd ed, 2013). A freely available resource is the Australian Style Manual, available at <https://www.stylemanual.gov.au/>.

This book is aimed at exactly that: *how* to go about engaging with the law and its relationship with the facts. The test is that the law you use must be *relevant*. This is a threshold test in evidence law and is equally applied to legal writing. Apply a modified version of the test for relevance.

> The law that is relevant in a question is law that, if it were accepted, could rationally affect (directly or indirectly) the assessment of the probability of the existence of a legal issue in the fact matrix.

By way of example, I once wrote an examination question for students that involved a waiter who was being paid cash-in-hand work at an event. During the evening, the waiter was drugged and sexually assaulted. One of the answers I received was that the issue was a breach of taxation laws for the unpaid work. The student completely missed the sexual assault. And while the response may have been a reasonably competent deployment of the *Taxation Administration Act 1953* (Cth), there was no mention of the *Crimes Act 1900* (NSW). The answer was fundamentally flawed. Technically, that answer was correct in the sense there *was* a legal issue present – but the student locked into the *wrong issue* because it was totally out of context and simply failed to answer the question.

Linked to this point is the need for *pinpoint* accuracy. Accuracy involves a combination of things. The law must be *current* (keeping in mind that in the criminal law complex cases can arise where people are prosecuted using legislation that has been repealed but was current at the time of the offence). Legislation is increasingly complicated, and it is not unusual for multiple but distinct matters to be contained within the same section. For example, in our discussion on GBH in Chapter 6, you will have seen that this offence is actually covered by different sections of the *Crimes Act 1900* (NSW). And within those sections there are different limbs, with different requirements and different consequences. So rather than talk about a person being liable for a charge under s 33, for instance, it would be better to be precise and say s 33(1)(b). That is a 'pinpoint' answer. It also goes without saying that the law must be *jurisdictionally correct*. I have had students who have cited provisions of law from the wrong state, and even the wrong country, in the process of their work. That happens because the student is using a word search on the internet, rather than actually reading and researching the relevant law.

Guiding principles

I call the following principles 'The Magnificent Seven'.

(1) The writing must be impeccable.
    (a) The document should be logically organised and structured.
    (b) Your sentences must be free from spelling and grammatical errors.
    (c) Pages should be numbered.

(2) The referencing must be consistent and precise. The standard referencing system in legal writing in Australia is set by the *Australian Guide to Legal Citation*, which you should follow.
(3) The law needs to be accurate, relevant, properly characterised, explained and applied.
(4) The issues identified need to be clear and related to the law.
(5) The reasoning/application of law to facts needs to be plausible, if not persuasive.
(6) Ambiguity, if present, should be resolved to the extent it can be.
(7) The research needs to be sufficiently detailed for the task.

RECOMMENDED READING

Nichola Corbett-Jarvis and Brendan Grigg, *Effective Legal Writing: A Practical Guide* (LexisNexis, 3rd ed, 2021).

John C Dernbach et al, *A Practical Guide to Legal Writing and Legal Method* (Wolters Kluwer, 7th ed, 2021).

Terry Hutchinson, *Researching and Writing in Law* (Lawbook Co, 4th ed, 2018).

Michael Meehan and Graham Tulluch, *Grammar for Lawyers* (LexisNexis, 3rd ed, 2013).

Terrill Pollman, Judith Stinson and Elizabeth Pollman, *Legal Writing* (Wolters Kluwer, 2nd ed, 2014).

APPENDIX A

HYPOTHETICAL EXAMPLE PROBLEM 1

Assume you are a solicitor working for Legal Aid. You have been approached by Eric McNamara, who is in possession of a court attendance notice, alleging that on 26 January 2020, he assaulted Floyd Jammal in Newcastle in the state of New South Wales, and recklessly caused grievous bodily harm.

The statement by the arresting officer, Constable Baldwin, indicated that he and another officer, Constable Jones, attended the Jade Garden Hotel on Hunter Street, Newcastle, at approximately 11 pm on 26 January. They did so in response to a call by security guards at that venue, advising that a serious fight had broken out between two patrons. When police arrived, they found that Eric had been detained by a security guard, and a man was being treated at the scene by ambulance officers. This was the victim, Floyd Jammal, who was being treated for head injuries. Police took statements from four witnesses who all stated that Eric had been drinking at the venue and was refused service by the bar manager. Eric became abusive and was asked to leave by security. He was then escorted off the premises. Eric began to argue with one of the security guards. Floyd was waiting in line to get into the bar. At one point he tried to calm the situation down by saying 'Look, mate, even I think you've had enough – why not just go home?' Eric turned his aggression towards Floyd, yelling 'It's none of your fucking business!' He then pushed his finger aggressively into Floyd's chest with sufficient force to cause him to step back. Floyd regained his footing and yelled 'Keep your hands to yourself, arsehole!' A fight then erupted.

CCTV footage from the door area of the bar captured most of the ensuing fight. There was an exchange of blows to the head and upper body of both men. At one point Floyd managed to knock Eric to the ground. At that time it appeared that the fight was over. Floyd then backed away. Eric got back to his feet, approached the victim and punched him on the side of the head, knocking him to the ground, where he remained. Eric was grabbed by two security guards and restrained until the police arrived.

Eric was arrested at the scene and taken to Newcastle Police Station. As he was intoxicated, he was kept in a cell overnight, and formally interviewed the following morning.

Photographs from the medical file, and the accompanying medical report, showed extensive bruising and abrasions to Floyd's hands, arms, upper body and face. On presentation to Big John Hospital, the victim was treated for a dislocated jaw. Subsequent medical reports indicate that Floyd was in a stable condition and recovering as expected, although he was consistently reporting anxiety and fear of public places as a result of the fight.

Personal information confirmed that Floyd is a 23-year-old university student, who worked part-time in a grocery store while attending college. He has been unable to return to work or study since the attack.

Eric is a 25-year-old accountant. He was a state ward and has no next-of-kin. He has five prior convictions for assault. These are all assaults that Eric committed on 26 January in the years he was 15 to 19 years of age. A psychologist report states that Eric reacted badly to his experience as a state ward, and during his adolescence he was largely uncontrollable. The link with 26 January was that his parents were killed in a motor vehicle accident on 25 January when he was seven years old. It seems that Eric drinks to excess on 26 January, and often becomes both melancholy and aggressive around this date.

On speaking with Eric, you learn that he managed to get into university to study accountancy and this made a huge difference to him. He could focus and find a 'purpose' and has been working as an accountant for the last three years. He had not been involved in any violence in recent years. He admitted to you that he drank 'at least' five schooners of beer on the day in question, but that he did not feel 'particularly drunk' – and that the trigger for him getting angry was the 'smarmy' way the bar manager had refused him service.

Discuss Eric's criminal liability.

APPENDIX B

HYPOTHETICAL EXAMPLE PROBLEM 1 GUIDED RESPONSE

Below is an example of how you might answer the hypothetical example problem in Appendix A. Like all things in law the answer presented here is not *the only* answer to the problem. It offers one example of style and a synthesis of the facts and law. You will note that the answer draws on some of the discussion in Chapter 6. It is an exercise in integrating relevant content into the write-up when the time comes. Remember that the write-up is the end of the process. It is the summary of your thinking on the problem, and the place where you should answer the question asked by the examiner. In this case the question is a broad one: 'Discuss Eric's criminal liability.' What follows is an informed discussion. A question of this kind is an open question. The key to a question like this is to consider the possibilities evident, and then select *the most likely* charge or charges based on the law and the facts. Importantly, you should be guided by the 'harm principle' – that is, if in doubt, focus on the most serious crime(s) that the law and the facts support. This is different to a closed question. A closed question might be 'Is Eric criminally liable for assaulting Floyd?', or a composite closed and open question, such as 'Has Eric caused grievous bodily harm to Floyd? If so, what charge or charges will he face?' Review Chapter 6, and then read the following and consider whether this response answers the question adequately and why.

Based on this information, Eric will likely be charged with one count of intentional infliction of grievous bodily harm ('GBH') pursuant to s 33(1)(b) of the *Crimes Act 1900* (NSW) ('*Crimes Act*'), with one count of assault occasioning actual bodily harm ('AGH') (*Crimes Act* s 59) or affray (*Crimes Act* s 93C) as viable alternatives. There is no defence apparent on the facts, with strong prosects of conviction. There are risks associated with a s 33 charge linked to the questions of intention and the nature of the injuries, so it is plausible Eric would not be convicted of a charge under s 33. The reasons are as follows.

Jurisdiction

The events the subject of the charge take place in Newcastle, New South Wales. All of the elements satisfying the charges take place within the geographic territory of New South Wales. As there is a geographic and factual connection between the elements of the offence and the state of New South Wales, the criminal law of that state applies.[1]

1 *Crimes Act 1900* (NSW) ss 10A, 10C.

There is no issue on this point, and the judge would take judicial notice of this.[2] There is no indication that any Commonwealth offence is involved.[3]

Age and state of mind

The facts do not state Eric's age, but clearly his is a 'natural person', and it is a fair assumption that as he was in a bar, he is over the age of 18. As the age of criminal responsibility in New South Wales is 10,[4] and there is no indication Eric is under 18, we can safely assume he is an adult and adult criminal responsibility and process applies. For the sake of completion, obtaining a copy of his birth certificate would be recommended, as there are different proceedings in New South Wales for offences committed by offenders under 18 years.[5] For the purposes of this discussion, we assume adult criminal responsibility.

There is no evidence Eric is labouring under some mental illness or similar condition that might otherwise excuse him from being held accountable or requiring diversion.[6] As will be discussed, there is some evidence of intoxication, but not at a level likely to affect his liability.

Intentional infliction of GBH?

The most serious charge in this scenario would relate to the consequences of the brawl between Eric and Floyd. Floyd suffered a dislocated jaw and ongoing psychological injury as a direct result of the altercation. A plausible charge resulting from that is an offence under s 33(1)(b) of the *Crimes Act*: intentional infliction of GBH.[7]

For Eric to be liable for that charge, the prosecution must establish the following:

(1) The injury suffered by Floyd was GBH, and
(2) Eric caused GBH, and
(3) Eric intended to cause GBH.

On the basis of the law and facts, it is safe to conclude there is no issue in relation to causation.[8] The injuries are categorically the result of the actions of Eric during that altercation with Floyd. The second element is clearly satisfied.

The threshold question is the nature of the injury. In New South Wales a 'grievous injury' has a common law meaning extended by a non-exhaustive definition in s 4.[9] That section includes the death of the foetus of a pregnant woman and causing grievous bodily disease, neither of which is presently relevant. GBH includes 'any permanent or serious

2 *Evidence Act 1995* (NSW) ss 143, 144.
3 *Criminal Code 1995* (Cth) ss 14, 15.
4 *Children (Criminal Proceedings) Act 1987* (NSW) s 10. It is noted that in respect of persons aged between 10 and 14, the common law doli incapax rule applies in New South Wales. See *BP; SW v R* [2006] NSWCCA 172; *R v CRH* (Unreported, NSWCCA, 18/12/96); *RP v The Queen* [2016] HCA 53; and more recently *BDO v The Queen* [2023] HCA 16.
5 *Children (Criminal Proceedings) Act 1987* (NSW).
6 *Mental Health and Cognitive Impairment Forensic Provisions Act 2020* (NSW).
7 *Crimes Act 1900* (NSW) s 33(1)(b).
8 An authoritative review of the various tests for causation is undertaken in *Royall v R* (1991) 172 CLR 378.
9 *Crimes Act 1900* (NSW) s 4.

disfiguring of the person'. At common law that requires the injuries be 'really serious'.[10] In this case the medical evidence documents 'extensive bruising and abrasions to Floyd's hands, arms, upper body and face', a 'dislocated jaw' and ongoing psychological injuries. The evidence also indicated that Floyd was 'recovering as expected'. This suggests the injury may not qualify as GBH, as it is not in the nature of a permanent or disfiguring injury, raising an issue as to whether the injury is ABH as opposed to GBH. In contrast, ABH 'means any hurt or injury that interferes with the health or comfort of a person. Such an injury does not need to be permanent, but it must have more than a fleeting or trivial effect upon the victim.'[11] In addition, it has also been held that psychiatric injury can constitute ABH, unlike GBH which is restricted to physical injury.[12]

In *Haoui v R*, McCullum J held 'the words "grievous bodily harm" ... do not require that the injury is a permanent one nor that the consequences of the injury are long-lasting or life threatening, but that they do require that the injury is a really serious one'.[13] This was approved in *Swan v R*.[14] In that case Garling J held that the distinction between ABH and GBH was one of 'fact and degree'. His Honour reviewed the authorities on GBH and concluded:

> [T]he following principles can be stated with respect to the phrase 'grievous bodily harm':
>
> **(a)** It is to be interpreted according to its natural and ordinary meaning;
> **(b)** On its natural and ordinary meaning, the phrase means not just serious bodily injury, but really serious bodily injury;
> **(c)** There is no bright-line by which an injury can be classified as really serious bodily injury; it is always a question of fact and degree;
> **(d)** Not every injury is capable of amounting to grievous bodily harm;
> **(e)** Only the injury itself and its direct physical effects, not its personal, social and economic consequences, can be taken into account in deciding whether an injury amounts to really serious bodily injury.[15]

The difficulty in this case is that the injury here may not be considered 'GBH'. It is certainly 'ABH', but whether it crosses the threshold in law to constitute 'GBH' is an open question to be determined in court. If it was concluded the injuries did *not* amount to a grievous injury, this charge would fail. As there is a good deal of certainty this injury would certainly qualify as ABH, a charge under s 59 is a viable alternative and would likely be nominated as a back-up charge.

A s 33(1)(b) charge is an offence of 'specific intent'. That is defined as 'an offence of which an intention to cause a specific result is an element'.[16] This means Eric's purpose in

10 *DPP v Smith* [1961] AC 290; *R v King* (2003) 59 NSWLR 472.
11 *Swan v R* [2016] NSWCCA 79, [56]. See also *R v Donovan* [1934] 2 KB 498 and *R v Brown* [1993] 2 WLR 556.
12 *R v Chan Fook* [1994] 1 WLR 691; *McIntyre v R* (2009) 198 A Crim R 549.
13 *R v Haoui* [2008] NSWCCA 209, [168].
14 *Swan v R* [2016] NSWCCA 79.
15 Ibid [71].
16 *Crimes Act 1900* (NSW) s 428B(1).

attacking Floyd was to inflict a grievous, or really serious, injury. 'Intention' is a term with ordinary meaning, related to the object or desire to produce a certain result through some act or omission.[17] The relevant period in which intention is considered is the totality of the incident, rather than a specific moment.[18] When the available facts are considered there is clearly evidence of very aggressive conduct, with a punch directed to the side of the head with enough force to knock the victim to the ground. There had been an exchange of blows to the head and upper body, combined with defensive wounds to the victim. Arguably, there is an inference available that Eric certainly intended to inflict physical injury. The question is whether it would be accepted that the intention was to inflict 'really serious injury'. If that was accepted by the court, then the relevant intention may be found. If not, then this element is absent, and the required level of intention would not be made it.

I would therefore suggest that while s 33(1)(b) is open on the facts, the problem with this charge if it was pursued is that the medical evidence may not establish the threshold for GBH has been established, *and* that proof of intention to cause that injury may not be established. As the burden of proof rests with the prosecution, and the standard of proof is beyond reasonable doubt,[19] this will be the main challenge for any prosecution of this section.

Alternative 1: Section 35

If the court was satisfied that a grievous injury was sustained, but that Eric did not have the specific intention to cause that level of injury, an alternative approach would be to rely on an alternative verdict available under s 33(3) of the *Crimes Act*.[20] That approach would mean the Crown could test the law and evidence in pursuing the most serious charge available on the facts and law.

Alternatively, preferring a charge under s 35(2) of the *Crimes Act* is also open on these facts. Section 35 is a composite offence containing charges linked to wounding and offences in company. There is no evidence of either wounding[21] or being in company,[22] so those options can be dismissed. The elements of a s 35(2) charge require:

(1) Floyd suffered GBH, and
(2) Eric caused GBH, and
(3) Eric was reckless in causing some bodily harm.

We have already discussed causation and GBH above. A s 35(2) charge carries with it the same risk that the medical evidence may not establish the injury is GBH. On the assumption it is, the mental element is *recklessness* as opposed to specific intention. Recklessness

17 See, eg, *Hyam v DPP (UK)* [1975] AC 55; *R v Moloney* [1985] AC 905; *He Kaw Teh v The Queen* (1985) 157 CLR 523.
18 *Sharp v R* [2012] NSWCCA 134.
19 *Evidence Act 1995* (NSW) s 141.
20 *Crimes Act 1900* (NSW) s 33(3).
21 A wound is a distinct injury characterised by a penetrating injury of the dermis and open bleeding. See *R v Shepherd* [2003] NSWCCA 351.
22 An offence 'in company' requires some combination of conduct and shared understanding or purpose between offenders. See *Brougham v R* (1986) 43 SASR 187, 191; *R v Button & Griffin* [2002] NSWCCA 159, [120]; *Markou v R* [2012] NSWCCA 64, [28].

is a term that is partially defined in the *Crimes Act* but characterised at common law. Broadly, recklessness can be established where the *accused foresees the possibility of the consequence and proceeds regardless*[23] – but this has an extended meaning by virtue of the definition in s 4A,[24] which includes intention and knowledge. In contrast to the high threshold required in s 33, it seems certain that Eric's purpose in the attack on Floyd was to at least inflict some injury, or that he foresaw the possibility he was going to inflict some harm, however fleeting. Section 35(2) is viable on these facts. There is no issue that Eric *caused* the injury to Floyd (element 2), but like the discussion on s 33, the issue here is whether the injury is GBH (element 1) and whether the prosecution can prove that Eric was reckless as to causing some injury (element 3). This is arguably easier for the prosecution, provided the court is satisfied the injury is grievous.

Alternative 2: Section 59(1)

An alternative approach that avoids the uncertainties within the key elements is a prosecution of assault occasioning ABH (*Crimes Act* s 59(1)). One option, as mentioned, is to charge s 59 as a specific alternative to the principal offence. The alternative position would be to charge Eric with one count of ABH pursuant to s 59(1). To be convicted of that charge, the prosecution would need to prove:

(1) Eric assaulted Floyd, and
(2) Floyd suffered ABH as a result.[25]

These elements are different to a charge under either s 33 or s 35, and if not researched carefully can be misleading. There is no statutory definition of assault in this section, and as such we must turn to the common law. At common law there is a distinction between assault and battery. The criminal law tends to use the term 'assault' interchangeably. The gist of an assault is some intentional or reckless act by the offender that causes the victim to 'apprehend immediate and unlawful harm'.[26] Battery involves intentional or reckless physical contact between the accused and the victim without consent, beyond physical contact in the 'exigencies of everyday life'.[27] Most authorities accept that the contact must involve both an element of force and be conducted in a manner that involves a degree of anger or hostility.[28] As a general rule, where there is consent to assault there is no assault as a matter of law.[29] However, there is clear authority that even when there is consent, those who engage in a fight are guilty of assault if they intend to inflict bodily harm.[30]

23 *Crabbe v The Queen* (1985) 156 CLR 464. Note there are some complex diversions arising because of the decisions in *R v Colosimo* (1990) 19 NSWLR 467 and *Blackwell v R* [2011] NSWCCA 93.
24 *Crimes Act 1900* (NSW) s 4A.
25 Ibid s 59(1).
26 *R v Knight* (1988) 35 A Crim R 314; *Zanker v Vartzokas* (1988) 34 A Crim R 11; *R v McIntyre* [2009] NSWCCA 305.
27 *Department of Health v JWB* (*'Marion's Case'*) (1992) 175 CLR 218.
28 There are innumerable cases on assault and battery. Leading authorities include *Fagan v Metropolitan Police Commissioner* [1969] 1 QB 439; *R v Phillips* [1971] ALR 740. Note in *Boughey v R* (1986) 161 CLR 10 it was held that hostility is not essential.
29 *R v Bonora* (1994) 35 NSWLR 74.
30 *AG Ref (No 6) of 1980* [1981] QB 715; *R v Raabe* (1984) 14 A Crim R 381.

In this case we are dealing with Eric physically hitting Floyd on multiple occasions. Those actions cannot be anything other than intended actions. The injuries that Floyd suffered have already been discussed above, and it seems unarguable that Floyd has suffered injuries that are *at least* within the meaning of ABH, and the direct cause of those injuries was the assault perpetrated by Eric. Unlike offences under s 33, a charge under s 59 is not an offence of specific intention. It is sufficient that the offender intentionally or recklessly assaulted the victim and ABH results.[31]

There seems little room to doubt that Eric would be convicted of this charge, either as an alternative charge to s 33 or s 35, or as a stand-alone offence. The weakness of this approach is that the charge may not satisfy the criminality involved. The maximum penalty for a s 59(1) charge is up to five years' imprisonment, as opposed to a charge under s 33, which carries up to 25 years. Given the prosecution is required to press charges in the public interest, consideration will need to be given to balance the prospects of conviction and the public interest, including the seriousness of the offending.[32]

Alternative 3: Affray (s 93C(1))

An alternative approach that does not rely on the injury as the basis for liability is an approach that relies on conduct. On such possibility is the charge of affray.[33] To convict Eric of this offence, the following elements would need to be proven:

(1) Eric used or threatened to use unlawful violence towards Floyd.
(2) That conduct was such that it would cause a person of 'reasonable firmness' present at the scene to fear for their safety.
(3) The conduct was intended, or Eric was aware his conduct may be violent.

Unlike the above offences that are concerned with characterisation of injury as key elements, affray is essentially concerned with a continuous course of conduct, based on participation of the accused in an uninterrupted melee. Thus, it is basically a fight over a period of time, which will involve multiple instances of intentional physical contact between two or more individuals, or threats of the same (often in the earlier stages). The accused must have intended the course of conduct or been aware their conduct might be violent.[34] That course of conduct must be such that it would cause the notional ordinary person who might be present to fear for his or her personal safety. This is an offence basically characterised by subjective and objective components. If satisfied the accused has either used violence (as defined)[35] towards another, and that their conduct is such that it would cause a person of reasonable firmness present to fear for their safety, then the offence is made out.[36]

31 *R v Coulter* (1987) 61 ALJR 537; *R v Williams* (1990) 50 A Crim R 213; *Crimes Act 1900* (NSW) s 428B.
32 Office of the Director of Public Prosecutions New South Wales, 'Chapter 1: The Decision to Prosecute', *Prosecution Guidelines* (Web Page, 29 March 2021) <https://www.odpp.nsw.gov.au/prosecution-guidance/prosecution-guidelines/chapter-1>.
33 *Crimes Act 1900* (NSW) s 93C.
34 Ibid s 93D.
35 Ibid s 93A.
36 The leading authority in New South Wales is *Colosimo v DPP* [2005] NSWSC 584, which considers a line of English authorities in conjunction with s 93C, affirming the principles set out above.

There is no doubt that Eric engaged in a sustained violent attack on Floyd. The leading authority, *Colosimo v DPP*,[37] confirmed the law requires us to look at the totality of the conduct as constituting the use or threatened use of force as a key element. There is no issue that is the case on the evidence available. The accused engaged in a sustained fight with the defendant, caught entirely on CCTV. There is no doubt this would demonstrate a continuous course of violent conduct necessary to satisfy the subjective physical element of the offence. There is no credible explanation other than the conduct was intended, and Eric was aware of the nature of the offending.

Regrettably, there is little in the way of case authority that establishes the scope of what is meant by a 'person of reasonable firmness', and equally little scholarly commentary on the meaning or scope of the term. The gist here is an objective test, determined by the tribunal of fact. The question is whether or not it would be open for a jury to conclude that a person of reasonable firmness, present at this event, would fear for their personal safety. On this evidence the answer is 'yes'. Police were called to the scene by local security, who clearly had difficulty in containing the ferocity of the incident. In these cases, it can be useful considering how you, as an individual, would feel in this situation. In the ordinary course of human experience people, as a rule, do not like to be present in the face of this kind of aggression, and routinely flee, or sometimes intervene. But fear is a very common and likely reaction, and therefore it would be open to conclude that a reasonable person would fear for their safety in this situation.

Defence 1: Self-defence?

Self-defence is a complete defence in New South Wales and is available if Eric can establish that (1) he believed the conduct was necessary to defend himself, and (2) that conduct was a reasonable response in the circumstances as he perceived them.[38] Given, however, that the accused was, in fact, the initial aggressor this seems unlikely. It should, however, be noted as a possible issue in the advice to be explored in more detail when and if the need arises. In New South Wales, self-defence has effectively been codified in s 418 of the *Crimes Act* and should be reviewed as part of the analysis, although, as suggested, the facts do not appear to support it. It is plausible the matter will be raised if it proceeds to trial, but as Eric was the aggressor in this case, and arguably his conduct was not reasonable in the circumstances, it would not likely succeed.

Defence 2: Intoxication?

In New South Wales intoxication is not a defence, but a matter relevant to the determination of whether or not a person was able to form the relevant state of mind needed for offences of specific intent. Intoxication is governed by pt 11A of the *Crimes Act*. It is a reference to the person being 'influenced by alcohol or drugs'.[39] We know from the

37 *Colosimo v DPP* [2005] NSWSC 584.

38 *Crimes Act 1900* (NSW) s 418. One of the leading cases on point is *R v Katarzynski* [2002] NSWSC 613. Cf the common law position expressed in *Zecevic v DPP* (1987) 162 CLR 645.

39 *Crimes Act 1900* (NSW) s 428A.

evidence the accused was present at the venue for the purpose of socialising and drinking. He did so willingly and in full knowledge of what he was doing. His intoxication is 'self-induced'.[40] Part 11A relies on a distinction between offences of 'general' and 'specific' intent, following the English decision of *R v Majewski*,[41] and the controversial decision of the High Court in *R v O'Connor*.[42] Here an offence of 'specific intent' is defined as 'an offence of which an intention to cause a specific result is an element'.[43] Section 33 is identified as such an offence. Sections 35, 59 and 93C are not so identified. Accordingly, pt 11A will only be of practical relevance if a charge under s 33 is preferred; otherwise, it has no application outside of the factual consideration and possibly in sentencing.

If the matter did proceed by way of s 33, then the intoxication question will need to be considered. While it is open to the accused to rely on intoxication, it would seem very unlikely that the level of intoxication evident on the facts would satisfy the degree of intoxication necessary in this case. The accused was clearly quite agile and aggressive in his conduct. On his own admission, he stated that he did not feel 'particularly drunk', although he had been refused service at the bar. As there is evidence of intoxication, there is a burden on the prosecution to prove, beyond reasonable doubt, that the accused had capacity to form, and in fact formed, the relevant intention (namely, to inflict serious injury). There does appear to be a degree of uncertainty in the law on this point. In *R v Makisi* the NSW Court of Criminal Appeal cautioned about the directions to be given in cases concerning intoxication.[44] Here a distinction was drawn between *capacity* and *formation* of intention. The central issue is concerned with the intention, as opposed to capacity – although the terms are linked. Capacity is linked to the ability of the person to reason. Formation is concerned with the outcome of a process of thinking. In the present case there does not seem to be a serious issue. The NSW *Criminal Trial Bench Book* model direction clearly advises that it is still open to the jury to find that a person may be well affected by alcohol, but still possess the relevant intention to injure another in that state. It is a matter of careful examination of the evidence.[45] In this case it would be open to the tribunal of fact to find the accused possessed the relevant intention, even in the presence of alcohol in his system.

Closing comment

There are no statutory limitation periods that apply to any of the offences being considered. Procedurally, depending on the preferred charges, this case could be dealt with summarily in the Local Court, which has important sentencing implications. The *Criminal Procedure Act 1986* (NSW) provides that ss 35 and 93C (Reckless infliction of GBH) are Table 1 offences. Such matters are dealt with summarily *unless* the prosecution

40 Ibid.
41 [1977] AC 443.
42 (1980) 146 CLR 64.
43 *Crimes Act 1900* (NSW) s 428B(1).
44 [2004] NSWCCA 333, [12]–[13].
45 Judicial Commission of New South Wales, 'Intoxication', *Criminal Trial Courts Bench Book – Trial Instructions H–Q* (Web Page, April 2023) <https://www.judcom.nsw.gov.au/publications/benchbks/criminal/intoxication.html>.

or the defence makes an election to proceed on indictment to trial.[46] Section 59 (Assault causing ABH) is a Table 2 offence. These matters are dealt with summarily *unless* the prosecution makes an election to proceed on indictment to trial. Section 33 (Intentional infliction of GBH) is not mentioned. Given the penalty is a maximum of 25 years, this is a 'strictly indictable offence', which means it must proceed to a jury trial. That requires the matter to have been referred to the DPP by the police for prosecution.[47] Should the matter be dealt with in the Local Court, the maximum penalty is up to two years' imprisonment, and/or a fine of 50–100 penalty units ($5500–$11,000).[48] In my opinion, the prudent course of action would be to charge Eric with an offence under s 33(1)(b), with a charge of s 59 in the alternative. The presence of an alternative verdict means that questions linked to mens rea can be adequately addressed through that mechanism, and any doubts about the extent of injury can be considered by the court. The matter would, therefore, likely proceed with the prosecution electing to proceed by way of indictment.

46 *Criminal Procedure Act 1986* (NSW) s 260.
47 See *Director of Public Prosecutions Act 1987* (NSW) pt 3.
48 *Criminal Procedure Act 1986* (NSW) ss 267–8; *Crimes Sentencing Procedure Act 1999* (NSW) s 17.

APPENDIX C

HYPOTHETICAL EXAMPLE PROBLEM 2 AND GUIDED RESPONSE

Ray Smith had been arrested by police after he was stopped for a random breath test while driving north to enjoy his 'annual leave' from a busy pharmacy practice. While conducting the breath test, Constable Spicer noticed an unusual smell coming from the rear of the car. Ray complied with Constable Spicer's direction to open the car boot; Constable Spicer found six empty large glass containers packaged safely inside the boot. Constable Spicer observed what he thought were scorch marks on the bottom of the containers. A carefully sealed glass jar containing approximately 185 mililitres of hypophosphorous acid was also located in the car boot. Ray told police that he had 'never seen the items before' and was stunned that they were in the boot of his car. An expert witness (forensic chemist) is available to give evidence that the heating of substances containing ephedrine or pseudoephedrine and later reaction with hypophosphorous acid is a method of manufacturing amphetamine favoured by Australian criminal groups.

Is Ray likely to face charges under the *Drug Misuse and Trafficking Act 1985* (NSW) in relation to these events?

On the assumption that Ray's drive 'north' was still within the boundary of New South Wales, the *Drug Misuse and Trafficking Act 1985* (NSW) ('DMTA') would apply. This is because there is a geographic nexus between offences contained in the DMTA, and the events described above.[1] Based on the facts we can infer that Ray is an adult (over 18 years of age), and therefore presumed to be criminally responsible.

The first matter to consider is whether the police officer was lawfully able to require a search of the vehicle, having pulled Ray over for a random breath test. If that search of the vehicle was unlawful, there is a risk that evidence of the subsequent search could be inadmissible.[2] It is therefore necessary to consider the legality of the search as a threshold issue.

Police officers have a general power to search persons and vehicles, without a warrant, pursuant to the *Law Enforcement (Powers and Responsibilities) Act 2002* (NSW).[3] These powers may be exercised without warrant where the officer 'suspects on reasonable grounds' that a person has in their possession anything connected with the commission of a 'relevant offence', or in connection with an offence under the DMTA. In

1 Part 1A of the *Crimes Act 1900* (NSW) applies to 'all offences' where the elements necessary to constitute an offence are committed wholly or partly within the state of New South Wales: *Crimes Act 1900* (NSW) ss 10A, 10C.
2 *Evidence Act 1995* (NSW) s 138.
3 Section 21 authorises a power to search persons; s 36 authorises a power to search vehicles.

George v Rockett,[4] the High Court held that this test was satisfied where there is evidence 'sufficient to induce belief or suspicion in the mind of a reasonable person'.[5] In other words, there must be some factual basis for the suspicion, but it need not be sufficient to establish a belief, much less proof. In a later case, in which the accused was pulled over by police and his vehicle searched for drugs (*R v Rondo*[6]), Smart AJ observed that 'reasonable suspicion is not arbitrary'.[7] In other words, it cannot be formed simply on conjecture. It is an evidence-based state of mind: 'a reasonable suspicion involves less than a reasonable belief but more than a possibility. There must be something that would create in the mind of a reasonable person [suspicion or belief].'[8]

In this instance, Constable Spicer's suspicions were aroused by the 'unusual smell' from the boot of the car. That is an objective fact, based on perception. It is also highly likely that an experienced police officer would have had prior experience of certain smells indicating the presence of drugs. Here the suspicion is based on direct perception that would have been available to the reasonable person. Accordingly, he had a lawful reason for requiring the car boot to be opened.

On these facts the most likely immediate charge would be found in s 24A of the DMTA. That offence prohibits the possession of apparatus and precursors intended by the accused to be used in the production of prohibited drugs or known by the accused to be used by another person.[9] This charge is the most likely, because mere possession of equipment is unlikely to constitute a charge of manufacturing prohibited drugs. In *R v BD*,[10] for example, the NSW Court of Criminal Appeal excluded such actions as being steps that are *preparatory* but not actual manufacture. It is therefore necessary to consider s 24A.

Section 24A(3) defines 'drug manufacture apparatus' and 'hypophosphorous acid' by reference to the Regulations. The *Drug Misuse and Trafficking Regulation 2011* (NSW) prescribes hypophosporous acid as a prohibited precursor.[11] Schedule 3 of the Regulations prescribes specific kinds of production apparatus, some of which are glass. Much would depend on the exact identity of the 'glass containers' in this case. If they are one of the identified kinds, then they are prohibited – otherwise they would not be.

Ray has the exclusive custody and physical control of glass containers and a jar of liquid. This constitutes the physical element of possession.[12] As Ray is the only person

4 (1990) 170 CLR 104.
5 Ibid [8].
6 [2001] NSWCCA 540.
7 Ibid [53].
8 Ibid. See also *Hyder v Cth* [2012] NSWCCA 336, where McColl J set out a lengthy framework after synthesising the authorities, including the above cases.
9 *Drug Misuse and Trafficking Act 1985* (NSW) s 24A.
10 (2001) 122 A Crim R 28. See also *R v Spicer* (2003) 139 A Crim R 206. Note that in *R v Marchione* (2002) 128 A Crim R 574 the decision in *BD* was distinguished in a case where the accused supplied Sudafed tablets to a co-accused in the knowledge that manufacture was going to take place. This was held to be within the meaning of manufacture under s 24 as the accused 'took part in a step of manufacture' in accordance with s 6.
11 Clause 5 sch 1.
12 Classically, see *DPP v Brooks* [1974] AC 862, where Lord Diplock held: 'In the ordinary use of the word "possession", one has in one's possession whatever is, to one's knowledge, physically in one's custody or under one's control.' This principle was accepted as correct in New South Wales by the Court of Criminal Appeal in 1976 in *R v Hinton* (Unreported, NSWCCA, 19 March 1976), and later by the High Court in *He Kaw The v The Queen* (1985) 157 CLR 523.

driving the vehicle, there is no issue linked to these objects being in the possession of another. Possession is, however, something that requires knowledge of the existence and nature of the object(s) in possession. In *He Kaw Teh*, Gibbs CJ, with whom Dawson and Mason JJ agreed, held that 'possession connotes knowledge of the existence of the thing possessed'.[13] In a separate judgment, Brennan J extended this somewhat, stating:

> On a count of possession [under the *Customs Act*] the onus is on the prosecution to prove that an accused, at the time when [they] had physical custody or control of narcotic goods, *knew of the existence and nature, or of the likely existence of likely nature,* of the narcotic goods in questions and that onus is discharged only by proof beyond reasonable doubt.[14]

To some extent the question of mens rea in drug cases is problematic, since a great deal depends on the interpretation of the specific words of legislation. In *R v Dib*[15] and *R v Greatorex,*[16] the NSW Court of Criminal Appeal held that the principles in *He Kaw Teh* also applied to the meaning of possession in the DMTA. There has been a tendency in judicial reasoning for an expanded approach to the state of mind in drug cases, particularly the more serious cases. For example, in *R v Baird*[17] the NSW Court of Criminal Appeal applied *He Kaw Teh,* and went on to conclude that it was sufficient if the prosecution proved the accused 'believed' the substance in possession was prohibited (in that case, cannabis). As shown above, the expansion of knowledge to include something less than actual knowledge was certainly endorsed by Brennan J – but it was also affirmed later in *Kural v R,*[18] and again in *Saad v R,*[19] where Mason CJ, Deane and Dawson stated:

> In a case such as the present where it is necessary to show an intention on the part of an accused to have in his possession a narcotic drug, that intent is established if the accused knew or was aware that an article which was intentionally in his possession comprised or contained a narcotic drug. That is not to say that actual knowledge or awareness is an essential element of the guilty mind required for the commission of the offence. It is only to say that knowledge or awareness is relevant to the existence of the necessary intent. Belief, falling short of actual knowledge, that the article comprised or contained a narcotic drug would obviously sustain an inference of intention. So also would proof of the possession of the forbidden drug in circumstances where it appears beyond reasonable doubt that the accused was aware of the likelihood, in the sense that there was a significant or real chance, that his conduct involved that act and he nevertheless persisted in that conduct. As a practical matter, the inference of mens rea or a guilty mind will ordinarily be irresistible in cases involving the possession of narcotic drugs if it is proved beyond reasonable doubt that the

13 *He Kaw The v The Queen* (1985) 157 CLR 523, 627.
14 Ibid 648 (emphasis added).
15 (1991) 52 A Crim R 64.
16 (1994) 74 A Crim R 496.
17 (1985) 3 NSWLR 331.
18 (1987) 70 ALR 658.
19 (1987) 70 ALR 667.

> accused was actually in possession of the drug and that he was aware, at the time of the alleged commission of the offence, of the likelihood of the existence of the substance in question in his possession and of the likelihood that it was a narcotic drug.[20]

The problem in the present case relates to the evidence of Ray's state of mind. Ray denies any knowledge of the existence of the materials. Denial of knowledge of the existence of the objects in the car necessarily denies any question of intention in relation to the use of the materials, and therefore makes the element of intention or knowledge of manufacturing equally problematic. Based on the authorities above it is clear that a properly instructed jury would find Ray was in the physical custody and control of these objects beyond reasonable doubt. However, the outcome in relation to Ray's state of mind is far from clear. As indicated in *Saad*, cases where a person is in actual custody of a narcotic will likely result in conviction if the Crown is able to establish some level of awareness as to something in the trunk of the car. Further, in *R v Pereira*[21] it was held that the threshold level of knowledge can also be established by evidence of a suspicious set of circumstances and the surrounding circumstances. However, a conclusion based on inferences must be carefully made: 'knowledge must be the only rational inference available'.[22]

In this case the hypothetical appears to be an extension of an investigation involving another accused also implicated in drug trafficking. We know from the first set of facts that Ray is a chemist. We also know that police 'had become aware' of an agreement relating to drug crimes involving Mark and Ray. Here we may assume that this information would form part of the evidence later presented in court relating to Ray's possession and knowledge of the manufacturing apparatus. As always, much would depend on the evidence available to the prosecution if the matter went to court, but it would appear that if all the information available in the first part of this case formed a part of the Crown case, then it would be open to the jury to infer the requisite level of knowledge. However, if the only material available is the mere possession of the objects, then the Crown case is not as strong.

An important consideration here is the fact that although offences arising under s 24A have a maximum penalty of 10 years' imprisonment and are indictable, they may be dealt with summarily in Local Court, as this is a Table 1 offence under the *Criminal Procedure Act 1986* (NSW).[23] Here the maximum penalty is limited to two years' imprisonment, or a fine of 100 penalty units,[24] or both.

20 Ibid [9].
21 (1989) 63 ALJR 1.
22 Ibid 3.
23 See s 260 sch 1 table 1 pt 6 cl 30A.
24 A penalty unit is $110. See *Crimes (Sentencing Procedure) Act 1999* (NSW) s 17. (The maximum fine would be $11,000.)

APPENDIX D

HYPOTHETICAL EXAMPLE PROBLEM 2: MEMORANDUM OF ADVICE IN THE MATTER OF *DPP V RAY SMITH*

In the following example, a different style of answer is presented. You should assume that the task was to provide a letter of advice. Specifically, the author was asked to provide a memorandum of advice to the Director of Public Prosecutions in the Ray Smith example. As a letter of advice, the style is rather different. You will note the document is more direct in its engagement with the client and the law. The client is another legal professional, who will likely require ready access to the law in making the decision to prosecute. Like all examples, it is not perfect. When reading this example, think about what you might do differently.

Introduction

(1) I have been asked for advice as to whether or not Ray Smith ('Smith') is likely to face charges under provisions of the *Drug Misuse and Trafficking Act 1985* (NSW) ('DMTA'). For the reasons that follow my advice is that, based on the current evidence, Smith **may** be liable for being in possession of drug manufacturing paraphernalia intended for use in manufacturing (DMTA s 24A), or liable for being in possession of prohibited precursor (DMTA s 24B). In my opinion, there is insufficient evidence to support a charge of manufacturing prohibited drugs (DMTA s 24). My instructing solicitor should advise immediately on any changes in available evidence.

(2) As detailed in the brief, Smith was arrested after police located a jar of hypophosphoric acid and various glass containers in the boot of his car, suggesting Smith was involved in the manufacture of amphetamines. The matter has since been referred to the DPP for advice on the likely charge or charges arising.

Threshold issues

Jurisdiction

(3) The brief does not detail exactly where Smith was arrested. On the assumption he was arrested in New South Wales, the DMTA will apply because there is a geographic nexus between offences contained in the DMTA, and the events

described above.[1] As he was driving, we may also infer that he is an adult, and therefore prima facie criminally responsible as a matter of law.

Lawful search?

(4) As a general proposition, for evidence to be admitted in a court it must be lawfully obtained.[2] It is therefore important to consider the legality of the search, given that Smith was pulled over for a random breath test.

(5) Police officers have a general power to search persons[3] and vehicles,[4] without a warrant, pursuant to the *Law Enforcement (Powers and Responsibilities) Act 2002* (NSW). These powers may be exercised without warrant where the officer 'suspects on reasonable grounds' that a person has in their possession anything connected with the commission of a 'relevant offence', or in connection with an offence under the DMTA.[5] 'Reasonable grounds' are considered in the common law. In *George v Rockett*,[6] the High Court held that this test was satisfied where there is evidence 'sufficient to induce belief or suspicion in the mind of a reasonable person'.[7] In other words, there must be some factual basis for the suspicion, but it need not be sufficient to establish a belief, much less proof. In a later case, in which the accused was pulled over by police and his vehicle searched for drugs (*R v Rondo*)[8], Smart AJ observed 'reasonable suspicion is not arbitrary'.[9] In other words, a search cannot be formed simply on conjecture. It is an evidence-based state of mind: 'a reasonable suspicion involves less than a reasonable belief but more than a possibility. There must be something that would create in the mind of a reasonable person [suspicion or belief].'[10]

(6) In this case it would be necessary to obtain a detailed statement from Constable Spicer. As noted above, the test is part subjective and part objective. We are here concerned with Spicer's reasons, compared with the hypothetical reasonable person. In this instance, Constable Spicer's suspicions were aroused by the 'unusual smell' from the boot of the car. That is an objective fact, based on perception. It is open to the jury to conclude that a reasonable person's curiosity may be aroused in that context. However, as evident in *R v Rondo* where a search is undertaken with insufficient suspicion, there is a risk that evidence flowing from the search may be rejected by the court as inadmissible.

1 Part 1A of the *Crimes Act 1900* (NSW) applies to 'all offences' where the elements necessary to constitute an offence are committed wholly or partly within the state of NSW: *Crimes Act 1900* (NSW) ss 10A, 10C.
2 *Evidence Act 1995* (NSW) s 138. See also *Bunning v Cross* (1978) 141 CLR 54; *R v Ridgeway* (1995) 184 CLR 19 for the position at common law.
3 *Law Enforcement (Powers and Responsibilities) Act 2002* (NSW) s 21.
4 Ibid s 36.
5 Ibid s 20.
6 (1990) 170 CLR 104.
7 Ibid [8].
8 [2001] NSWCCA 540.
9 Ibid [53].
10 Ibid. See also *Hyder v Cth* [2012] NSWCCA 336, where McColl J set out a lengthy framework after synthesising the authorities, including the above cases.

Offences pursuant to the DMTA

Manufacturing?

(7) The facts suggest a link between Smith and the manufacturing of prohibited drugs. It is highly unlikely these facts would sustain a charge of this kind. In *R v BD*[11] the accused was found to be in possession of 27,000 Sudafed tablets and glassware, strongly indicating his involvement in manufacturing. Here the NSW Court of Criminal Appeal upheld his appeal against conviction for manufacturing and entered a verdict of acquittal.[12] The Court did so on the basis that mere possession and transportation of implements, without more, was not a 'step in the process of manufacture' as required by the Act.[13] As there is no evidence in the present brief as to more than possession and transportation, this avenue is not advised.

Possession of precursors and apparatus for manufacturing

(8) Section 24A of the DMTA prohibits the possession of precursors and apparatus intended or known by the accused to be used for the purpose of manufacturing a prohibited drug.[14] In the alternative, it is an offence under s 24B merely to be in possession of precursors used in the manufacture of a prohibited drug, whether known by the accused or not.[15]

(9) There are two threshold issues here, linked to the nature of the substance and the glassware. Hypophosphoric acid is a prescribed precursor,[16] and as such there is no issue that its possession is an element in any offence. Glass containers, however, may not be. Schedule 3 of the Regulations prescribes specific

11 (2001) 122 A Crim R 28.

12 *R v BD* (2001) 122 A Crim R 28. Justice Bell, with whom Stein JA and James J agreed, held (at 32): 'To my mind the acquisition and/or transport of chemicals or equipment do not, without more, constitute steps in the process of manufacture. They are steps merely preparatory to the process of manufacture.' See also *R v Spicer* [2003] NSWCCA 108; *R v Kaddour* [2005] NSWCCA 303. Note, in *R v Parker* (2002) 132 A Crim R 413 it was found that popping blister packs did amount to a step in the process.

13 Relevantly, s 24(1) of the DMTA provides: 'A person who manufactures or produces, or who knowingly takes part in the manufacture or production of, a prohibited drug is guilty of an offence.'

14 *Drug Misuse and Trafficking Act 1985* (NSW) s 24A 'Possession of precursors and certain apparatus for manufacture or production of prohibited drugs: (1) A person who has possession of: (a) a precursor, or (b) a drug manufacture apparatus, intended by the person for use in the manufacture or production, by that person or another person, of a prohibited drug is guilty of an offence.'

15 Ibid s 24B 'Possession of prohibited drug precursors: (1) A person who has in his or her possession a precursor of a quantity not less than the quantity prescribed by the regulations in relation to that precursor is guilty of an offence. (2) It is a defence to a prosecution for an offence under subsection (1) if the defendant establishes: (a) that the defendant is in possession of the precursor for the purposes of an activity that is not unlawful, or (b) that the defendant otherwise has a reasonable excuse for possessing the precursor. (3) In this section, precursor means a substance: (a) that is capable of being used to manufacture or produce a prohibited drug, and (b) that is specified or described in the regulations as a precursor for the purposes of this section.'

16 Ibid s 24A(3); *Drug Misuse and Trafficking Regulations 2011* (NSW) cl 5 sch 1.

kinds of production apparatus, some of which are glass. Much would depend on the exact identity of the 'glass containers' in this case. If they are one of the identified kinds, then they are prohibited – otherwise they would not be. It will be necessary to specifically identify these containers, otherwise their possession is not unlawful.

(10) Both offences under the DMTA require, as a matter of law, that Smith be 'in possession' of the prescribed objects. In addition, to be liable under s 24A it must be established beyond reasonable doubt that Smith either intended to use these materials in the manufacture of a prohibited drug, or for another to do so.

(11) Physical possession does not appear to be an issue in this case. Ray has the exclusive custody and physical control of the containers and precursor. This constitutes the physical element of possession.[17] As Ray is the only person driving the vehicle, there is no issue linked to these objects being in the possession of another.

(12) Possession is, however, something that requires knowledge of the existence and nature of the object(s) in possession. In *He Kaw Teh*, Gibbs CJ, with whom Dawson and Mason JJ agreed, held that 'possession connotes knowledge of the existence of the thing possessed'.[18] In a separate judgment, Brennan J extended this somewhat, stating:

> On a count of possession [under the *Customs Act*] the onus is on the prosecution to prove that an accused, at the time when [he/she] had physical custody or control of narcotic goods, *knew of the existence and nature, or of the likely existence of likely nature*, of the narcotic goods in questions and that onus is discharged only by proof beyond reasonable doubt.[19]

(13) To some extent the question of mens rea in drug cases is problematic, since a great deal depends on the interpretation of the specific words of legislation. In *R v Dib*[20] and *R v Greatorex*,[21] the NSW Court of Criminal Appeal held that the principles in *He Kaw Teh* also applied to the meaning of possession in the DMTA. There has been a tendency in judicial reasoning for an expanded approach to the state of mind in drug cases, particularly the more serious cases. For example, in *R v Baird*[22] the NSW Court of Criminal Appeal applied *He Kaw Teh*, and went on to conclude that it was sufficient if the prosecution proved the accused 'believed' the substance in possession was prohibited (in that case, cannabis). As shown above, the expansion of knowledge to include something less than actual

17 Classically, see *DPP v Brooks* [1974] AC 862, where Lord Diplock held: 'In the ordinary use of the word "possession", one has in one's possession whatever is, to one's knowledge, physically in one's custody or under one's control.' This principle was accepted as correct in New South Wales by the Court of Criminal Appeal in 1976 in *R v Hinton* (Unreported, NSWCCA, 19 March 1976), and later the High Court in *He Kaw Teh v The Queen* (1985) 157 CLR 523.

18 *He Kaw The v The Queen* (1985) 157 CLR 523, 627.

19 Ibid 648 (emphasis added).

20 (1991) 52 A Crim R 64.

21 (1994) 74 A Crim R 496.

22 (1985) 3 NSWLR 331.

knowledge was certainly endorsed by Brennan J, later affirmed in *Kural v R*,[23] and again in *Saad v R*.[24]

(14) In *Saad*, Mason CJ, Deane and Dawson affirmed their view that the state of mind of the accused may be inferred from the surrounding facts, concluding:

> As a practical matter, the inference of mens rea or a guilty mind will ordinarily be irresistible in cases involving the possession of narcotic drugs if it is proved beyond reasonable doubt that the accused was actually in possession of the drug and that he was aware, at the time of the alleged commission of the offence, of the likelihood of the existence of the substance in question in his possession and of the likelihood that it was a narcotic drug.[25]

(15) The difficulty in the present case is that Smith (perhaps incredulously) has denied any knowledge of the contents of the car boot at all. Denial of knowledge of the existence of the objects in the car necessarily denies any question of intention in relation to the use of the materials for manufacturing (which compromises both a charge pursuant to ss 24A and 24B). Based on the authorities above, it is clear that a properly instructed jury would find Ray was in the physical custody and control of these objects, but the question of his state of mind is far from clear. Courts have, however, indicated a willingness to treat such cases with an open mind. In *R v Pereira*[26] it was held that the threshold level of knowledge can also be established by evidence of a suspicious set of circumstances and the surrounding circumstances. However, a conclusion based on inferences must be carefully made: 'knowledge must be the only rational inference available'.[27] Ultimately it will be a question of fact for the jury should it proceed to trial, although it certainly presents a risk to the prosecution of a charge under s 24A.

(16) The situation may be clearer, however, if the evidence of a related investigation is available to the prosecution. It appears that another party is also implicated in drug trafficking. We know from the brief that Ray is a chemist. As always, much would depend on the evidence available to the prosecution if the matter went to court.

(17) On the present information it is my opinion that Smith should be charged with possession of a prohibited precursor only, pursuant to s 24B. Although this charge is technically a Table 1 offence[28] that carries a maximum penalty of five years' imprisonment and/or a fine of 1000 penalty units,[29] this is a case where the matter would be dealt with summarily.

23 (1987) 70 ALR 658.
24 (1987) 70 ALR 667.
25 Ibid [9].
26 (1989) 63 ALJR 1.
27 Ibid 3.
28 *Criminal Procedure Act 1986* (NSW). See s 260 sch 1 table 1 cl 30B.
29 *Drug Misuse and Trafficking Act 1985* (NSW) s 33AB.

INDEX

accuracy of law, 9
acronyms, for basic principles of problem solving, 2–3
actual bodily harm ('ABH'), 78–9, 95
actus reus, 12, 20, 72
affidavits, 31
affray, 72, 75–6, 79, 85–6
age of criminal responsibility, 21
analysis, *see* legal analysis; problem analysis
Aristotelian philosophy, 58–9
assault
  consent, 85
  definition, 78
  elements, 84
  occasioning actual bodily harm, *see* actual bodily harm ('ABH')
  occasioning grievous bodily harm, *see* grievous bodily harm ('GBH')

balance of probabilities, 38–40
battery, 78
beyond reasonable doubt, 38, 40–1
burden of proof, 26, 35–7

causation, 13
chronologies, 61
circumstantial evidence, 33–5
CLEO, 2
common law rights/liberties, 49–50
conditional law, 21
consent, 85
constitutional law, 25
CRARC, 2
Crimes Act 1900 (NSW), 69
  pt 3, 71
  pt 11A, 89, 90
  s 4, 82
  s 33, 71, 73, 76–7, 84, 87, 88, 90, 91, 93, 96
  s 33(1), 71, 73, 77
  s 33(2), 73
  s 35, 71, 73–4, 77–8, 84, 87, 89–91, 94, 96
  s 35(2), 71, 95
  s 59, 71, 75, 84, 90, 91, 94–6
  s 93C, 72, 75–6, 85, 90, 91, 94, 96
  s 93C(1), 76
  s 93D, 76
  s 93D(2), 79
  s 418, 91
  s 428C, 90
Crimes (Sentencing Procedure) Act 1999 (NSW), 47, 69, 95
criminal justice process, phases of, 92
Criminal Procedure Act 1986 (NSW), 69, 93
culpability, establishing, 16–17, 19

defences
  determining possible defences, 64
  grievous bodily harm, 89–91
  intoxication, 89–91
  self-defence, 91
  validity of, 15
double jeopardy, 92

elements of offences
  actus reus, 12, 20, 72
  ancillary concepts, 17
  contextual elements, 12
  essential elements, 12
  fault elements, 18, 51, 52
  hidden in surrounding legalities, 14, 19–21
  identifying, 9, 24–5, 61–2, 72–6
  mens rea, 12, 20, 72
  mental elements, 20, 51–3
  operative concepts, 17
  physical elements, 18, 20
  qualifying/procedural elements, 18
epistemic knowledge, 58
ethical practice, 5–6
evidence
  admissibility, 24, 28, 64
  affidavits, 31
  believability, 33–5
  categories of reporting, 32–5
  circumstantial evidence, 33–5
  direct experience of witnesses, 32
  documentary evidence, 30, 70
  establishment of liability and culpability, 16–17
  expert reports, 30

evidence (*cont.*)
  hearsay evidence, 30, 33
  identifying, 62, 79–82
  indirect experience of witnesses, 32
  medical evidence, 70
  oral testimony of witnesses, 30–5
  perception and reliability, 33–5
  physical evidence, 30
  relationship with law, 8–9
  relevance, 27–8
  reliability, 24, 33–5
  role of, 15–16
  satisfying legal elements, 19
  scepticism, 26–7
  sources, 30
  weight of, 28–9
evidence law, 17

facts
  applying to law, or applying law to, 59–60, 68
  material facts, 57
  matters in issue, 25–6
factual uncertainties, 63, 86–9

grievous bodily harm ('GBH')
  affray and, 75–6, 79, 85–6
  age of accused, 69
  alternative charges, 91
  application of law to facts, 68
  association and evaluation of elements and evidence, 82–6
  categorisation of offence, 93–4
  in company, 78, 81, 83
  consent, 85
  defences, 89–91
  definition, 77, 82
  elements of offence, 72–6
  evidence, identification of, 79–82
  factual uncertainties, 86–9
  harms, identification of, 70–1
  injury, 76–8, 80, 82–3
  jurisdiction, 68–9
  legal uncertainties, 89
  limitation periods, 93
  possible outcomes of charge, 95–6
  preliminary interpretation, 76–9
  procedural considerations, 92–4
  recklessness, 77–8, 89
  relevant law in NSW, 69
  scoping the law, 71–2
  sentencing, 94–5
  specific intent, 77, 90
  state of mind, 69, 80–1
  statutory alternative verdict, 91

hearsay evidence, 30, 33

iceberg principle, 13–15
identification of accused, 70–1
ILAC, 55
indictable offences, 47
intoxication, as defence, 89–91
IRAC, 2, 3

judicial reasoning, 2, 55
jurisdiction, 60, 68–9
justice, and law, 59

larceny, 17–21
law
  accuracy of sources, 9
  as applied predictive discipline, 7–8
  as discipline of potentialities, 3
  depth required, 9–11
  empirical foundations, 7
  justice and, 59
  relationship with evidence, 8–9
  relevance to task at hand, 10, 11
Law Enforcement (Powers and Responsibilities) Act 2002 (NSW), 69
legal analysis
  guiding principles, 8
  see also problem analysis
legal personality, 12, 69
legal reasoning
  flaws in, 4–5
  forms, 3
  iceberg principle, 13–15
  nature of, 55
  non-judicial legal reasoning, 8
  unethical practice, 5–6
legal uncertainties, 89
liability
  absolute liability, 54
  establishing, 16–17, 20, 72
  scoping the law, 61

- strict liability, 53
- unpacking a discussion question on, 56

limitation periods, 15, 49, 93

mens rea, 12, 20, 51–3, 72
MIRAT, 55, 56

offences
- against the person, 69
- categorisation of, 93–4
- public order offences, 72
- *see also* elements of offences; *specific offences, eg* assault

operative terms, 8
outcome decisions, 8

penal statutes, 44
penalties
- limits on, 46–9
- penalty units, 21
- statutory maximum penalties, 13

Phillips v R [2016] NSWCCA 159, 83
phronetic knowledge, 58
police powers, regulation, 69
pre-trial police processes, 64
private law, 25
problem analysis
- advanced model, 55, 58–9
- alternatives, 64, 91
- applying law to facts, or facts to law, 59–60, 68
- associate and evaluate elements and evidence, 62–3, 82–6
- basic model, 55–8
- categorisation of offence, 64, 93–4
- chronologies, 61
- conclusion and advice, 66–7, 95–6
- defences, 64
- elements, identication of, 61–2, 72–6
- empirical foundation, 56
- evidence, identification of, 62
- factual uncertainties, 63, 86–9
- harms, identification of, 60–1, 70–1
- issues, 56–7
- jurisdiction, 60, 68–9
- legal uncertainties, 63, 89
- material facts, 57
- phronetic approach, 58–9
- preliminary interpretation, 62, 76–9
- procedural considerations, 64, 92–4
- procedures required, 60–1, 70–1
- rules, 58
- scoping the law, 61, 71–2
- sentencing issues, 65–6, 94–5

problem solving
- acronyms of basic principals, 2–3, 55
- art of, 2, 55
- CLEO model, 2
- CRARC model, 2
- ILAC model, 55
- IRAC model, 2, 3
- logical progression, 66
- MIRAT model, 2

procedural law, 17, 25, 61, 69
process decisions, 8
public order offences, 72

reasoning, *see* judicial reasoning; legal reasoning
reckless grievous bodily harm, 11–13
relevant law, 2, 7, 9, 10, 48, 58

scepticism, 26–7
self-defence, 91
sentencing, 65–6, 69, 94–5
specific intent, 77, 90
standard of proof
- balance of probabilities, 38–40
- beyond reasonable doubt, 38, 40–1
- civil proceedings, 38–9
- criminal proceedings, 38–41
- overview, 38–40

statutory interpretation
- basic example, 11–13
- categories of terms in legislation, 43–4
- common law rights/liberties, 49–50
- general principles, 42–4
- Interpretation Acts, 44–5
- limits on penalties, 46–9
- penal statutes, 44
- retrospectivity, 50–1
- special rules and principles, 45
- strict interpretation, 45–6

substantive law, 61
summary matters, 47
Summary Offences Act 1988 (NSW), 72
- s 11A, 79

uncertainty
factual uncertainties, 63, 86–9
legal uncertainties, 89

violent disorder, 72

witnesses
direct experience, 32
expert evidence, 30
indirect experience, 32
oral testimony, 30–5

For EU product safety concerns, contact us at Calle de José Abascal, 56–1°, 28003 Madrid, Spain or eugpsr@cambridge.org.

www.ingramcontent.com/pod-product-compliance
Ingram Content Group UK Ltd.
Pitfield, Milton Keynes, MK11 3LW, UK
UKHW051258040726
472853UK00011B/618